The Seller-Doer Playbook

Unlocking Business Development Skills for Design Professionals to Accelerate Your Career Growth

Bradley Waldrop, P.E.

Waldrop Communications

Copyright ©2024 by Bradley Waldrop

All rights reserved.

No portion of this book may be reproduced in any form without written permission from the publisher or author, except as permitted by U.S. copyright law.

Contents

1. Unlock the Secrets to Winning Even the Toughest Projects with "The Seller-Doer Playbook"!   1
2. Introducing The Seller-Doer Playbook   3
3. My Journey to Success in the Seller-Doer Arena   6
4. The Motivation Behind a Billion-Dollar Framework   10
5. Identifying the Benefits for the Next Generation   14
6. The Critical Shift for Design Professionals   19
7. Debunking Myths: Young Professionals and the Sales Mindset   24
8. Understanding the Seller-Doer Mindset for New Professionals   29
9. Building a Foundation for Business Development Success   34
10. Spotting Opportunities   38
11. Winning Strategies   43
12. The Art of Extraction   48
13. Building Relationships Beyond Transactions   53
14. Crafting Proposals That Shine   58

15.	The Power of Storytelling in Business Development	63
16.	Communicate to Connect	67
17.	Avoiding Pitfalls in the Sales Cycle	71
18.	The Lifelong Value of Follow-Ups in Client Relations	76
19.	Measuring Success in Business Development	80
20.	Collaboration as a Catalyst for Enhanced Sales Efforts	84
21.	Balancing Act	90
22.	Showcasing Seller-Doer Value	94
23.	Top Three Actionable Takeaways for Immediate Impact	99
24.	The Future of Business Development in Engineering and Construction	104
25.	Thriving as a Seller-Doer	110
26.	Unlock Your Proposal Success with Our FREE Cheat Sheet!	115

Chapter One

Unlock the Secrets to Winning Even the Toughest Projects with "The Seller-Doer Playbook"!

In an industry marked by fierce competition and political complexities, **Bradley Waldrop** has distilled years of hard-won experience into this indispensable guide for design engineers like you. He wrote "*The Seller-Doer Playbook*" to empower up-and-coming professionals with the tools, strategies, and insights needed to craft proposals that not only win projects but redefine success in your career.

With an impressive track record of selling nearly **$1 billion in professional services**, Bradley knows what it takes to navigate the intricacies of project proposals and client relationships. He has been a key player in more **once-in-a-lifetime projects than he cares to count**, delivering over **$8 billion in constructed infrastructure** along the way. His extensive leadership roles, including serving as the Membership Committee Chair and Public Works Institute Co-Chair for the American Public Works Association, and as the Past President of both the Sacramento Capital Branch and Sacramento Section of the American Society of Civil Engineers, further validate his expertise. As an Industry Mentor for CE 191 Senior Project at California State University, Sacramento, Bradley is dedicated to shaping the next generation of civil engineers, ensuring they have the skills and insights needed to succeed.

Now is your moment! Dive into *"The Seller-Doer Playbook"* and let Bradley's wealth of knowledge guide you through the complexities of proposal crafting. Uncover how to stack the deck in your favor and catapult your career to new heights. **Start reading today**—the victory you've been aiming for is just a page away!

Chapter Two

Introducing The Seller-Doer Playbook

Congratulations on your purchase of *The Seller-Doer Playbook*! You're holding in your hands not just a book, but the key to unlocking unparalleled success in your design engineering career. I crafted this guide with a singular mission: to arm you with the tools and insights needed to craft winning proposals that can catapult you into the upper echelons of your field.

As an up-and-coming design engineer, you've already honed your technical skills through rigorous education and practice. But let's face it—how many hours did you spend learning about the intricacies of business development and sales in college? If you're like most professionals in our field, the answer is probably "not enough," or "none." This gap often means that, despite your hard work and talent, it could take up to 15 years before you see the fruits of your labor in winning projects. Imagine being able to compress that timeline, skyrocketing your chances of success from the outset.

In *The Seller-Doer Playbook*, I'm excited to share a proven framework that has been instrumental in my career, culminating in nearly $1,000,000,000 in professional engineering and construction management services sold. Throughout my 35 years in this industry, I've navigated the complexities of proposal crafting and client relationships. Now, I want to pass those hard-won lessons on to you.

This isn't about spending endless hours building relationships or taking clients out for unproductive lunches. Instead, my goal is to guide you toward making strategic choices that will maximize your efficiency and effectiveness as a seller-doer. You'll gain insights into how to stack the deck in your favor, even on the most politically charged or difficult projects. Understanding the nuances of what clients crave and how to meet those needs through your proposals can significantly differentiate you from your peers.

Throughout the pages of this book, you'll find easy-to-follow techniques and tips that I battle-tested for you in the real world. I designed it to be practical and applicable, allowing you to take immediate action. By the end of your journey through these chapters, you'll have clarity on what makes up the most effective use of your time and resources in the enchanting yet often bewildering realm of sales and business development.

As a civil engineer who has stood at the crossroads of creativity, strategy, and execution, I promise that the knowledge in *The Seller-Doer Playbook* will set you up not just as a doer of engineering tasks but as a seller of solutions that clients genuinely desire.

So go ahead—dive into your book! Each page is waiting to equip you with insights that could redefine your approach to clients and proposals. I hope you finish with a robust framework that propels you towards the success you envision for yourself. Remember, the journey may seem daunting, but with the right knowledge and strategy, you can chart a path that leads to remarkable achievements.

Here's to turning your aspirations into realities—one proposal at a time! Happy reading!

Chapter Three

My Journey to Success in the Seller-Doer Arena

In the early 1990s, the landscape of civil engineering was taking a hit as the market experienced a significant downturn. Picture a junior engineer—like me—navigating this challenging environment, armed with technical skills and a passion for entrepreneurship, but confined to the daily grind of drafting and designing. Many professionals were simply trying to weather the storm, focusing on perfecting their engineering skills. However, I quickly learned that to stay relevant and successfully keep a job, I needed to adapt.

I noticed that many engineers around me were struggling not just to find work, but to forge connections in the business world. Instead of solely diving deeper into technical work, I recognized an opportunity to diversify my skill set. My natural inclination was towards technology, and I had a solid understanding of computer systems and graphics. This knowledge led me to assist in proposal writing and creating visual graphics to support our proposals. It was a pivotal moment; I was no longer just an engineer—I carved out a niche as someone who could help bridge the gap between technical expertise and business development.

During this time, I wasn't responsible for delivering the technical content of our proposals nor the management of schedules. My role was more focused on the "nuts and bolts" of crafting proposals and helping the company present our capabilities in the best light possible. Balancing my time between engineering work, IT support, and marketing taught me invaluable lessons. I became familiar with the proposal process from multiple angles, setting the stage for my future success. By observing both winning and losing proposals, I identified patterns that contributed to winning.

These observations became the bedrock of my approach in the seller-doer arena. As I immersed myself in the proposal process, I fine-tuned my understanding of what makes a proposal compelling. I learned to highlight strengths, address client needs, and present ideas engagingly. Over time, I established key principles that not only helped me win work but also became a framework that I applied as my career progressed.

Eventually, the economy rebounded, and as businesses flourished, I found myself in a fortunate position. I had developed a unique skill set that allowed me to win my own work. This was a transformative experience for me, as I implemented the strategies I had refined during the downturn. No longer was I mere support in the background; I was at the forefront, competing against established teams that had long been favored for projects.

Entering the proposal process armed with the principles I'd honed; I would quickly assemble a winning team. My understanding of how to structure a competitive advantage became my guiding light. I approached interviews not only with facts and figures, but with a narrative that resonated with clients. The art of storytelling became integral to my method. I learned to connect with the selection committee on a human level, understanding their needs and aligning our skills to meet those requirements.

This ability to connect has had a significant impact on my success. As the years went by, my winning rate soared; I saw tangible results. The dollar amounts involved were significant, amounting to nearly $1 billion in professional services over my career. This included various roles in design, construction management, public outreach, and more—all within both private and public sectors. Each successful proposal reinforced the process I had developed, providing me with even more confidence and refining my skills further.

What became clear through my journey is that even individuals with a purely technical background could thrive in a sales-oriented environment without coming across as pushy or disingenuous. By focusing on authentic connections and transparent communication, I turned the stereotype of the used car salesman on its head. I was not a salesperson in the traditional sense, but a problem solver who could provide value to clients.

The key takeaway from my journey is that the transition from technical expert to valued seller-doer is achievable for anyone willing to learn and adapt. Embrace your technical skills while simultaneously honing your ability to communicate effectively. In this approach, you can still maintain your authentic self and build meaningful relationships with clients that highlight your expertise without compromising your integrity.

As you reflect on this chapter of my journey, I hope you see that there's a clear pathway for highly technical professionals like yourself to become effective seller-doers. With determination, adaptability, and a focus on communication, you too can thrive in the competitive landscape of engineering and sales. It's not only about selling services; it's about sharing your expertise and making lasting connections that lead to mutual success. Your journey might just be beginning, and the possibilities are endless.

Chapter Summary:

- Diversify your skills: Learn proposal writing and marketing to complement your engineering expertise.

- Observe and analyze: Study successful proposals to identify winning strategies and patterns.

- Connect authentically: Build meaningful relationships with clients through transparent communication and storytelling.

- Embrace adaptability: Combine your technical skills with effective sales techniques to enhance your career.

Chapter Four

The Motivation Behind a Billion-Dollar Framework

In the fast-paced world of design and business, understanding the sales cycle is crucial. Many skilled professionals excel in their technical abilities but struggle with selling their services or ideas. This chapter addresses a significant turning point—a framework that can transform how you view sales, venturing beyond numbers and logic into the realm of emotional intelligence and communication.

The motivation behind developing this framework stems from a shared frustration: many design professionals are good at what they do, yet they often learned through trial and error. Think of it like riding a bike. You can practice until your legs ache, but if you haven't learned how to balance, you'll keep falling over. This framework provides the balance you need—writing down lessons learned to create a foundation that anyone on your team can understand and use effectively.

The first element to grasp is the importance of communication. For many technically skilled individuals, the focus has been on hard analytical skills, which seem black and white, with clear right or wrong answers. However, in the real world, especially in sales, it's less about geometric identities, physics principles, and mathematical equations. It is more about how to convey your ideas. Here is where effective communication comes into play.

Picture your communication skills like a key to unlock a door. If you possess the key (skills) but don't know how to use it or the door in front of you (the opportunity), you will remain stuck. The framework emphasizes not only mastering technical proficiency but also honing the ability to tell compelling stories. When you craft your narrative well, you inspire trust, connection, and confidence in clients.

It's crucial to recognize the emotional capabilities that come into play during sales conversations. Technical professionals often operate in a landscape of data and logic, believing that facts will sell themselves. However, clients often decide based on how they feel. For instance, if a client feels understood and appreciated through your interactions, they are more likely to choose you for their project—not just on the strength of your technical prowess, but because of the relationship you've built.

Another pivotal aspect of the framework is the idea of building a team that embodies this approach. Why is this so important? When a team operates from the same foundational structure, their collective understanding fosters collaboration. It's no longer about one person working hard; it's about a cohesive unit that sells as a team. Picture a sports team; they achieve success not just because each player is highly skilled individually, but because they learn how to work together and expect each other's moves.

As you develop your communication and emotional skills, it becomes essential to practice soft sales skills daily. This means finding opportunities to engage with clients in ways that build rapport, express empathy, and communicate value—all of which can transform a conversation. Imagine a consultation session where you listen deeply to a client's concerns while also elaborating on how your design can solve their problems. This is the essence of selling work through understanding and connection.

With these practices in mind, you begin to shift the narrative. Rather than seeing sales as a daunting task reserved for a select few, you recognize that it's a skill set that anyone can learn. Developing this framework encourages you to take control of your destiny, transforming you into a "seller-doer." This term refers to professionals who actively engage in sales while also doing the work that they sell, ensuring that they maintain a strong connection to both clients and the projects that emerge.

As you internalize these concepts and put them into practice, you find that your value within your organization increases. Your peers will view you as an invaluable asset, not just for your design skills, but for your ability to convey ideas and engage clients. You'll find that your work becomes not just a job, but a journey of self-discovery and empowerment.

Now, reflecting on the larger picture, this framework is just as applicable personally as it is professionally. By honing your approach to emotional intelligence, communication, and relationship-building, you position yourself not only to advance in your current role but also to take risks in pursuing new opportunities. Perhaps you could even venture out on your own one day, leveraging this framework to build your own client base and driven team.

In conclusion, by taking the lessons within this chapter to heart, you can undertake the journey towards extraordinary value creation. Through mastering both technical skills and soft sales techniques, not only will you enhance your career, but you will empower those around you as well. By fostering a culture of collaboration and communication within your team, you can reshape not just your own destiny, but the future of your organization. Embrace this framework, and you may just find that the sky is the limit.

Chapter Summary:

- Master communication and storytelling to engage clients and build trust.

- Practice soft sales skills to enhance client rapport and express empathy.

- Foster team collaboration to transform individual efforts into collective success.

- Embrace emotional intelligence to boost your value and career opportunities.

Chapter Five

Identifying the Benefits for the Next Generation

In today's rapidly changing landscape, up-and-coming design professionals and engineers are stepping into roles that not only require technical prowess but also an understanding of business development and sales. We will explore who will benefit most from this vital skill set in this chapter, and we will discuss how you can use these insights to take control of your career.

Imagine you're an architect, sitting at your desk, designing an innovative building. While the act of designing is crucial, what if that project was only half of your potential? As a novice in the design profession, merely delivering projects is no longer enough. You should strive to become a "seller-doer," which means actively engaging in both delivering the project and securing it.

Who Can Benefit?

The first group poised to benefit immensely is the next generation of engineers and design professionals like yourself. If you're eager to take control of your journey and future, learning to secure your projects is essential. You'll be able to pursue work that excites you while collaborating with clients that resonate with your values. This is not just about holding onto your current tasks, but crafting a fulfilling career filled with meaningful projects.

Consider this: when you own your work pipeline, you steer your career in the direction you desire. Imagine landing a project that excites you—an architectural wonder or a groundbreaking engineering solution. Learning the essentials of business development can help you grasp these opportunities, moving beyond the routine of projects that simply land on your desk.

The Pressure of the Seller-Doer Role

Next, let's talk about individuals thrust into the sales side of their design firms. Maybe you're feeling the pressing need to bring in work to maintain job security and feed your family. This can be overwhelming, but you're far from alone. Many talented professionals find themselves in uncomfortable positions where they must learn to sell their services effectively.

Understanding the fundamentals of business development can reduce that anxiety. By breaking it down into manageable steps—selling your services, presenting proposals, and negotiating terms—you can develop the skills needed to thrive in this dual role. When you do, not only will you survive, but you'll also excel, securing work that values your skills and aligns with your passions.

The Entrepreneurial Spirit

The third group this chapter speaks to includes individuals with an entrepreneurial drive. Perhaps you've been eyeing the possibility of starting a new group in your existing firm or even launching your own business. With a good idea and tenacity, you're already halfway there! Yet, many professionals in this position often lack the structure to turn their visions into reality.

To succeed in this endeavor, you require a solid framework for creating successful proposals and understanding the business development side of your industry. You'll want to learn the steps needed to go from a big idea to a solid opportunity. The process includes everything from identifying potential projects, crafting proposals, interviewing, negotiating scopes, and finally executing the work.

Moving Beyond Chaos

Think of the process as navigating a map with various roads. Without a defined pathway, it's easy to become lost or overwhelmed. However, with the right framework, dealing with intricate business development processes becomes less daunting. It helps you move through chaos and turn your vision into reality systematically.

By establishing a robust business development strategy, you can reach out to the right clients, pitch compelling proposals, and secure rewarding projects. This makes not only your career fulfilling but also your professional journey much more enjoyable. You'll no longer have to fumble through an ambiguous process. Instead, you can be strategic and intentional in your approach, leading to more satisfying outcomes.

The Role of Curiosity

One of the best aspects of learning about business development, marketing, and sales is that it taps into your innate curiosity. Your training as a design professional has already equipped you to observe, analyze, and innovate. By channeling that curiosity into understanding the dynamics of business, you will find that connecting with clients and selling your ideas becomes easier and more natural.

Curiosity helps you better understand your clients' needs, allowing you to craft solutions that truly resonate with them. This connection not only makes you invaluable but also enhances the relationships you build in your career. A curious mindset can pave fresh paths for you and spark conversations that may lead to unexpected opportunities.

Taking Control of Your Career

Even if you haven't received formal training in sales or marketing, know that your inquisitive nature is your greatest asset. Harness it! As you learn and grow in these areas, you will discover valuable skills that empower you to steer your career in the direction you desire. Remember, you have the potential to create a fulfilling and successful professional life.

By taking the time to understand and cultivate these skills, you will position yourself as a key player in your organization and the industry at large. You will not only be known for delivering outstanding projects, but you'll also be recognized for your ability to win work that aligns with your passions.

Your Path to Value and Success

In conclusion, there are immense benefits for the next generation of design professionals willing to embrace business development and sales as part of their toolkit. Whether you're a novice looking to craft a fulfilling career, a seller-doer facing the pressure of immediate sales needs, or an ambitious entrepreneur aiming to launch your vision, understanding this framework is paramount.

Even though you may feel you're not trained in these areas, remember that your natural curiosity can be your guiding compass. Embrace it, learn, and apply these principles to take control of your career. As you become more valuable to your team and clients, the opportunities in your path will flourish, leading to a rewarding and influential career. So rise to the occasion, and shape your future today!

Chapter Summary:

- Embrace the "seller-doer" mindset to secure desirable projects and career growth.

- Learn fundamental business development skills to empower your professional journey.

- Cultivate curiosity to connect with clients and enhance your value in the field.

- Take proactive steps to shape your career and unlock rewarding opportunities.

Chapter Six

The Critical Shift for Design Professionals

As an up-and-coming design professional, you may have been told that your primary responsibilities are purely technical. While honing your design skills is undeniably important, there is a critical shift that you must embrace: understanding and taking part in business development and sales. This chapter will demystify the world of business development, reinforcing that sales is not just for the extroverted or the experienced. Rather, it's a vital part of your role that can elevate your career and make you an invaluable asset to any team.

Understanding the Importance of Business Development

Let's begin with a simple truth: sales and marketing are everybody's job. This may initially sound surprising, but consider this—if you're producing great work, communicating well, and nurturing your client relationships, you are already part of the business development cycle.

Your talent and dedication will naturally attract opportunities if you handle these basics effectively. Remember, a project starts well before the contracts are signed; it begins with how you present yourself, your work, and your ideas.

Taking Control of Your Workload

Many design professionals feel frustrated when they are required to simply follow orders. We all want to work on projects that excite us and allow us to express our creativity. Embracing business development gives you the power to identify opportunities. With this shift, you won't just be waiting for assignments; you will actively hunt for projects that inspire you and align with your vision. This shift can transform your career from reactive to proactive, leading to a more satisfying professional life.

The Art of Finding Opportunities

The first step in the business development process is learning how to find opportunities. Start by networking within your industry. Attend local design events or online webinars where you can meet potential clients and collaborators. Don't underestimate the value of casual conversations—often, the most lucrative opportunities arise from informal discussions. Use your existing network to seek referrals, take part in community projects, or even collaborate with freelancers.

Turning Opportunities into Projects

Once you identify potential opportunities, your next challenge is turning them into projects. This is where your technical skills meet your organizational savvy. Begin by ensuring you fully understand the client's needs. Ask clarifying questions and show that you listen. Delivering customized and thoughtful responses will position you as a problem solver. Clients will see you not just as a technical worker, but also as a partner who can help them reach their goals.

Building Your Reputation

By proactively seeking opportunities and addressing clients' needs, you find that your reputation as a "seller-doer" grows. This term might sound unfamiliar, but it's simply a way of describing someone who both creates and sells. As you and your team complete projects successfully and clients see your dedication, word of mouth will help you. Remember, when you deliver quality work and treat clients well, they become your best advocates, bringing in more business opportunities.

Developing Sales Skills

You might be thinking, "I didn't sign up for sales," but fear not! Selling doesn't mean being pushy or overly aggressive. Instead, think of sales as relationship-building. Familiarize yourself with basic sales tactics, such as the art of persuasion and effective communication. Practice creating compelling pitches and proposals. What makes your design approach unique? How can it solve a client's problem? Learn to articulate these points clearly.

Learning Through Experience

Just like design, the skills needed for business development improve over time. The more you practice, the more comfortable you'll become. Start small—perhaps start a discussion with an existing client about future work or propose ideas for new projects. You can hone your ability to sell your services in each interaction, while also getting a sense of how your ideas are being received.

Achieving Financial Independence

As you grow more adept at finding and winning projects, a new world of financial possibilities opens. With the ability to attract your own work, you can demand higher pay and even consider starting your own practice. By assuming a leadership role in your projects and taking charge of your workload, you position yourself not just as an expert, but as a go-to person within your industry.

Building a Leader's Mindset

Being a design professional who embraces business development naturally fosters a mindset of leadership. You become a mover and shaker—a problem solver who can navigate complex workflows and client demands with ease. Such skills make you more than just a designer; they empower you to influence the direction of your projects and your organization, making you a recognized leader in the field.

Delivering Results

Successful delivery of projects is the ultimate goal of business development, and winning projects is just the first step. Every successful project builds your track record and enhances your credibility. Showcase your completed projects using a portfolio that not only highlights your design skills but also speaks to your involvement in securing and managing those projects. The more projects you complete successfully, the more sought-after you'll become in your industry.

Shifting Your Focus for Career Growth

As you reflect on your journey, it's essential to recognize that you already possess the technical skills necessary for an outstanding career in design. Now, it's time to pivot your focus toward business development and marketing. This mindset will not only enhance your ability to navigate the business side of design, but also position you as a vital contributor to your team's success.

A New Era in Your Career

In summary, the journey from being a technically skilled designer to a proactive seller-doer isn't as daunting as it seems. By embracing business development and sales, you're not just taking charge of your workload—you're crafting a fulfilling career path filled with opportunities. Expand your scope and tap into the potential that already resides within you. With each opportunity tackled and each project won, you become a cornerstone of your organization, ready to shape your career on your own terms.

Chapter Summary:

- **Embrace business development** to transform your role from order-taker to project seeker.

- **Network actively** to discover new opportunities through events and informal conversations.

- **Build relationships** by understanding client needs and delivering customized solutions.

- **Develop sales skills** gradually, starting with small conversations to boost confidence.

Chapter Seven

Debunking Myths: Young Professionals and the Sales Mindset

In the world of design, creativity, and technical skills reign supreme. Young professionals often find themselves immersed in the core elements of their craft—whether it's mastering the latest design software or understanding the principles of structural integrity. However, for selling their services and driving business development, many feel a sudden jolt of apprehension. This chapter explores common misconceptions that may hold young design professionals back from embracing the sales mindset.

One of the most pervasive myths is the idea that "I can't do it." This notion suggests that training in math and science makes you incapable of excelling in sales. This belief is not only misleading but can lead to a detrimental mindset that stifles growth. The reality is that being a good designer often means being a good problem solver. Whether you are crafting a design or selling your services, both tasks rely on your ability to address challenges effectively.

Another misconception that is common among young professionals is the stereotype of the "slick" salesperson. The image of the used car salesman, complete with charm and questionable ethics, often clouds young designers' perceptions of what sales can be. In truth, successful selling is about genuine communication and relationship-building rather than flashy pitches or manipulation. Think of it this way: just as you collaborate with colleagues on a design project, engaging clients in meaningful conversations can lead to successful business outcomes.

Some might believe that you need decades of experience to be effective in sales. However, let's dispel this myth. Even young professionals with the right mindset and willingness to learn can excel in business development. Many industries value fresh perspectives and new ideas that come from bright, emerging talents. Your insights as a proficient designer can resonate with clients seeking innovative solutions, and your age could be an asset rather than a liability.

"I'm not a project manager, so I can't sell" is another misconception that can hinder young professionals. This belief positions sales as the sole responsibility of those at the helm of a project. Every team member, from entry-level designers to seasoned managers, holds potential as a seller. Each of you communicates with clients and understands their needs, which is crucial in the sales process. By being proactive and contributing to discussions about projects, you establish your credibility and showcase your value.

Some young design professionals may feel that the decorative aspects of a proposal—often referred to as "fluff"—are the main focus when it comes to selling. However, while presentation matters to some extent, the substance of what you offer is far more important. Clients are primarily interested in solutions to their problems and how your skills can meet their needs. Therefore, focus on building a narrative around the value you bring rather than solely on presentations that may prioritize style over substance.

Another commonly held belief is that you must be an absolute expert in every technology related to your project to be an effective seller. This couldn't be further from the truth. While technical abilities are important, what truly sets you apart is your capacity to understand the client's needs and articulate how you can provide a solution. Being knowledgeable in your field is essential, but you don't need to have mastered every single tool to deliver a compelling pitch. Instead, focus on highlighting your strengths and how your unique approach can solve the client's problems.

The misconception that you can't be both a creative and a promoter is a pervasive barrier. Many young professionals have been trained to view their roles as distinct: designers create, while salespeople sell. This division, however, isn't necessary. In fact, many successful design firms thrive when their designers embrace the sales cycle as part of their roles. By practicing your narrative skills and positioning yourself as a problem solver, you can bridge the gap between design and business development.

Another myth revolves around the idea that formal sales training is essential for success in business development. Although courses and programs are available, many successful individuals in sales learn through experience. Don't underestimate the valuable skills you've gained through team projects and client interactions. Every conversation and collaborative effort contribute to your learning. By reflecting on these experiences, recognize that you already possess many tools to effectively engage in the business aspects of your career.

Building relationships is a core component of sales, yet young professionals often overlook this area. Many feel that the business development process is too formal or transactional. Effective selling is about forging connections. These relationships can open doors for professional opportunities, repeat business, and referrals. Think of your network as a living tapestry—each interaction strengthens the threads, contributing to a greater tapestry of experiences and opportunities.

As young professionals, you also carry a fresh perspective that can be highly valuable to potential clients. People in positions of authority and experience sometimes fall into stagnant patterns and ideas, missing new trends or solutions. Your voice, creativity, and innovative approaches can challenge the status quo. Embrace your position as a budding professional; your unique outlook can significantly enhance business development efforts.

In summation, understanding and overcoming these misconceptions surrounding sales is pivotal for young design professionals. Embrace the truth that you possess valuable skills and perspectives that uniquely qualify you to engage in business development. As you break free from limiting beliefs, you will not only elevate your own career but also enhance the value you bring to your team.

In a world where effective business development and marketing are rare, your willingness to embrace this powerful and uncommon skill set amplifies your importance within the design field. Doing so transforms you into an invaluable seller-doer who is not only a creative thinker but also a compelling advocate for your work. As you navigate your career, remember that the ability to sell is not just about closing deals; it's about creating meaningful connections and solving genuine problems for your clients. Embrace this mindset, and you will thrive in a competitive landscape.

Chapter Summary:

- Challenge the belief that you can't excel in sales as a designer.

- Shift focus from flashy pitches to genuine communication and relationship-building.

- Recognize that everyone, regardless of role, can contribute to the sales process.

- Leverage your fresh perspective and experiences to enhance business development efforts.

Chapter Eight

Understanding the Seller-Doer Mindset for New Professionals

In the world of design and engineering, being successful goes beyond just applying technical skills. Now, more than ever, up-and-coming design professionals must embrace the "Seller-Doer" mindset. But what does this term really mean? At its core, a Seller-Doer is someone who not only delivers quality projects but also engages in activities that help secure future work. It's about being proactive and taking ownership of your career. In this chapter, we will break down the concept of a Seller-Doer, explore its importance, and outline how you can adopt this mindset for a more rewarding career.

What is a Seller-Doer?

Imagine you're not just a talented engineer or designer sitting behind a desk, crunching numbers or creating plans. Picture yourself as someone who wears two hats: one for delivering high-quality work and another for marketing those skills to attract new projects. A Seller-Doer operates at this intersection, performing important business development tasks while executing the core functions of their role. This holistic approach means that you can influence your workload while also contributing to your organization's growth.

Why is the Seller-Doer Mindset Important?

The construction and design industries are competitive, and new opportunities can be hard to come by. For new professionals, adopting a Seller-Doer mindset can transform your career trajectory. When you shift your focus from simply completing tasks to also understanding and solving your customer's biggest problems, you position yourself as a valuable asset. This dual role not only enhances your credibility but also opens doors to new projects, and, in many cases, establishes long-term relationships with clients.

Taking Ownership of Your Future

One of the most significant benefits of being a Seller-Doer is taking control over your professional future. As a young professional, it's easy to feel like a cog in a wheel, merely executing assigned tasks without any input on who gets the next job. However, when you adopt the Seller-Doer mindset, you actively take part in business development activities that can shape your career path. This proactive stance lets you focus on projects that inspire you, instead of passively waiting for tasks to come your way.

Multiple Hats, Multiple Skills

In a typical day, a Seller-Doer wears multiple hats. On one side, they might be involved in the technical aspects—whether it's running calculations, managing projects, or conducting quality reviews. On the other side, they are equally engaged in business development tasks. This might include networking, participating in client meetings, or even preparing proposals. By developing skills in both areas, you become more versatile, making you more indispensable to your organization.

The Team's Victory is Your Victory

As a Seller-Doer, your contributions are crucial to the team's success. When you secure new projects, everyone in the organization benefits—from your colleagues who will work on the project to the leadership that views your contributions favorably. Your ability to bring in work translates to more opportunities and growth for your team, making you an integral part of the organization's future.

Being Instrumental and Innovative

Embracing the Seller-Doer mindset allows you to be instrumental in your organization. It offers the chance to not only take part in existing projects but to innovate—coming up with new solutions that can solve client problems more effectively. This capability can lead to new types of work that may not have been explored before, positioning you as a thought leader in your field.

Control Over Your Work and Team Dynamics

Taking on the Seller-Doer role also offers a sense of control over the projects you undertake. When you are engaged in business development, you have the opportunity to select work that aligns with your interests and strengths. This enhances job satisfaction and makes it easier to build a work environment where your colleagues also thrive. You're setting the stage for a supportive atmosphere, where everyone enjoys what they do.

Expanding Your Experience

The dual focus of being a Seller-Doer allows you to expand your experience more rapidly than if you were to focus solely on technical execution. Business development requires you to engage with clients and understand their needs. This interaction provides invaluable insights that can improve both your technical work and business acumen. Over time, these experiences will enrich your career and establish your reputation as a knowledgeable professional.

Training Others in the Process

As you grow into your Seller-Doer role, you'll also have opportunities to mentor colleagues and help them take on similar responsibilities. Sharing your knowledge not only enriches your work culture but also establishes you as a leader in your organization. When your peers see how much you contribute, they are likely to follow your lead, creating a thriving environment where everyone shares the responsibility of business development.

Work-Life Balance and Personal Satisfaction

There's a personal benefit to adopting the Seller-Doer mindset as well. With increased control over your projects and work activities, you can maintain a healthier work-life balance. Engaging in diverse tasks brings variety to your workday, which can reduce burnout and enhance job satisfaction. As you take charge of your projects, you align your work with your values and goals, leading to greater personal fulfillment.

Your Transition from Doer to Seller-Doer

To sum it up, the Seller-Doer mindset is no longer a nice-to-have; it's a vital component of success in today's competitive industry landscape. By shifting your focus from delivery to actively solving client problems, you are setting the stage for a fulfilling and successful career. Embrace the mindset of a Seller-Doer, and unlock doors that turn you from a task-doer into a valuable asset, giving you the power to shape your own professional journey.

Chapter Summary:

- Embrace the Seller-Doer mindset for a proactive and fulfilling career.

- Balance technical skills with business development activities to add value.

- Actively take part in client interactions to expand your experience and credibility.

- Mentor colleagues to foster a collaborative business development culture.

Chapter Nine

Building a Foundation for Business Development Success

Emerging design professionals must embrace a broader role as "seller-doers." This dual identity — both a talented designer and a proactive business developer — can distinguish you in a competitive marketplace. In this chapter, we will uncover the foundational skills and knowledge areas that are critical for your business development success.

It's essential to understand that the foundation of your career is rooted in the business itself. Unlike product-based industries, design is primarily a service-oriented endeavor. It involves a relationship between you, your team, and your client, who is ultimately the one funding your work. Therefore, focusing on delivering high-quality work is paramount. Understanding how your work adds value and how it ties back to the financial success of your business is fundamental. Can you articulate how your projects will not only meet but exceed client expectations? This clarity sets the stage for productive discussions and successful outcomes.

Knowing your client is another cornerstone for business development. Who are they? Where do they congregate, be it online or in person? These questions are essential. Define your ideal client by considering who you want to work with. What projects do they typically engage in, and what budget do they allocate for these endeavors? Understand their preferences for hiring consultants or teams. The more specific you can be in identifying your client, the better you can tailor your approach to meet their needs.

But it's not just about knowing your clients; it's also about understanding the value you bring to them. What problems do you solve uniquely? This is where your differentiators become important. For example, are you exceptionally skilled at a certain design software that others in your field are not? Or do you have a background in a unique niche of design that allows you to meet specific client needs? Understanding and communicating these differences will help you create a compelling case for why clients should choose you over your competitors.

Next, consider the partnerships that can enhance your business development efforts. Identifying potential collaborators can expand your offerings and strengthen your value proposition. Ask yourself: Who can help you deliver more comprehensive services? Are there consultants or specialists you could team up with to bolster your skill set? By forming strategic alliances, you can enhance the quality and scope of your work, ultimately benefiting your clients.

Alongside partnerships, embrace the core values and technological advancements within your practice. Decide what innovations you want to integrate into your design processes. Are you looking at new design software, sustainable materials, or cutting-edge methodologies? Keeping abreast of technological changes will not only make your work more efficient but also enable you to offer state-of-the-art solutions to clients, thus making you even more valuable.

An often-overlooked but vital skill in business development is curiosity. As a design professional, you likely possess an innate desire to understand the world around you. Harness this natural curiosity and redirect it toward your clients and their needs. Explore their motivations and challenges. This not only deepens your understanding but also builds rapport. By engaging with clients at a deeper level, you will find more opportunities to offer value.

This curiosity mirrors the scientific method in design: creating a hypothesis about what a client needs, testing it through dialogue and feedback, and adapting your solution based on insights gained. By using this iterative approach, you can refine your understanding of client needs and continuously improve the relevant solutions you propose.

Remember, the skills to be a successful seller-doer might differ greatly from the technical prowess you've developed in school. They are not about finding the perfect words or mastering the latest sales techniques. Instead, they are practical, foundational skills focused on understanding and meeting client needs. Anyone can learn them, regardless of their background.

Your path as a seller-doer is an evolutionary journey. It starts with a clear understanding of the business dynamics at play and the needs of your clients. Identify what sets you apart, seek collaborative opportunities, and remain curious about the people you serve.

By following these foundational steps, you will not only enrich your career but also ensure that you are seen as an invaluable contributor in your industry. The most successful seller-doers leverage their natural curiosity to build meaningful relationships, leading to long-term success.

In conclusion, if you combine your design skills with these essential business development capabilities, you'll set yourself up for a fruitful career. Focus on understanding your client, recognizing your unique value, forming vital partnerships, and maintaining a curiosity about the people you serve. With dedication and the right approach, you can become a standout seller-doer in the design world.

Chapter Summary:

- Understand the client relationship: Know who they are and what they need.

- Communicate your unique value: Articulate how your skills solve client problems.

- Build strategic partnerships: Collaborate to enhance services and broaden your offerings.

- Embrace curiosity: Explore client motivations for deeper connections and tailored solutions.

Chapter Ten

Spotting Opportunities

In the world of design professionals, identifying opportunities within your network is essential for career growth and success. Whether you're an architect, engineer, or a designer, your ability to understand and discover these opportunities can elevate your work from merely executing projects to being an invaluable partner in the business development and sales cycle. In this chapter, we'll explore practical steps you can take to leverage your network and cast a broader net for future projects.

Step 1: Understand Project Planning

Every successful project begins with planning, and understanding this foundational concept is crucial. Clients don't just wake up and decide to build a new facility or renovate an existing one. They have a vision and a roadmap that guides them. This requires you to be inquisitive—start by researching project owners within your network or related industries. Ask questions that dig deeper into their plans. What are their short-term and long-term goals? This knowledge creates a solid groundwork for identifying what opportunities may arise.

Step 2: Join Professional Associations

Networking is about relationships, and professional associations are brilliant venues for building them. If you're not already part of relevant organizations, now is the time to join. Whether it's architecture, engineering, or design-focused groups, these associations provide access to valuable contacts and information about upcoming projects. Don't just attend meetings passively; involve yourself. Volunteer for committees or boards. Participation in these settings allows you to connect with other professionals who might have information about future projects.

Step 3: Engage in Conversations

Being present at meetings and events is just half the battle. Engage actively in conversations! Don't stick to small talk; ask thoughtful questions that show your genuine interest. For instance, if someone mentions a project, ask about the challenges they foresee, or what innovations they are considering. This curiosity not only helps you gather useful information but also positions you as someone who truly cares about the industry. Such interactions can reveal hints about potential opportunities.

Step 4: Conduct Thorough Research

Much of the information you need is available through public sources. Many projects are documented in magazines, shareholder reports, and public notices. Dedicate time to dig into this data. Learn how public agencies compile improvement plans—these often include future projects lined up for development. Make a habit of researching relevant publications or online resources. Understanding market trends will help you expect where these opportunities may arise.

Step 5: Build Relationships with Clients

Once you identify potential clients that align with your career hopes, reach out and ask them non-intrusive questions about their future plans. Clients appreciate vendors who show interest in what they are planning. They often love to share projections, and even if some information is confidential, you'll undoubtedly gain insights that can inform your strategy. Remember, the goal here is to establish yourself as an interested partner rather than just a service provider.

Step 6: Identify Key Decision-Makers

Within any organization, there are specific individuals who drive project decisions. Research who these decision-makers are and work on building relationships with them. You can often find this information via LinkedIn or professional networks. Understanding their needs and challenges will help to tailor your approach, making it easier to pitch how your services can solve their problems and advance their goals.

Step 7: Establish a Supportive Team

Collaborating with the right partners is vital to creating a competitive edge. Sit down with your contacts and discuss your findings, share ideas, and probe them for their insights into future projects. Successful partnerships often stem from mutual trust and knowledge sharing. If someone hesitates to share information or you feel uncomfortable sharing your own, this might signal that you need to reassess that partnership.

Step 8: Analyze Your Competition

As you navigate through opportunities, understanding your competition is crucial. Identify what sets you apart and how you can excel in securing contracts. Look for competitors who may not conduct thorough research or foster meaningful connections. This understanding will allow you to distinguish your offerings and show how your skills and insights make you the best choice for the projects at hand.

Step 9: Create a Shortlist of Opportunities

Once you've gathered enough information, create a shortlist of potential projects that resonate with your professional skills. This shouldn't be just any list—focus on projects where your services can add considerable value. Align your skills with project needs and compile a list that has a higher likelihood of turning into contracts.

Step 10: Monitor and Be Proactive

The landscape of potential projects fluctuates, and staying informed is key to spotting new opportunities. Regularly check in on industry news, project updates, and any shifts in your network. Be proactive in your discussions; if you identify changes that might affect a client's needs, adapt your strategy accordingly to fit those needs.

Step 11: Persist and Follow Up

Networking consistently leads to positive results. Sometimes opportunities won't materialize right away; relationships take time to develop. Don't hesitate to follow up after initial conversations or meetings. A simple "check-in" can keep your name on their radar when future projects arise.

Taking Control of Your Network

In conclusion, to move from being a passive design professional to an active participant in the business development and sales cycle, you must step out of your comfort zone. Your network is not just a collection of contacts; it's a goldmine of opportunities waiting to be tapped. Whether through associations, conversations, or diligent research, every interaction is an opportunity to learn and identify the challenges your clients face. Be attentive to their needs and be prepared to offer solutions. When you embrace a proactive approach, you'll find that the possibilities for collaboration and success are abundant.

Remember, it's all about building those connections and being genuinely interested in the people you work with—this is where genuine opportunities begin.

Chapter Summary:

- Research project owners in your network to uncover potential opportunities.

- Join professional associations to expand your network and access valuable information.

- Engage actively in conversations to gather insights and show genuine interest.

- Create a shortlist of opportunities that align with your skills for focused outreach.

Chapter Eleven

Winning Strategies

Understanding the likelihood of winning a project is crucial for design professionals who want to be seen as an invaluable part of the business development and sales cycle. It allows them to take control of their workload and enhance their value to the client. In this chapter, we will break down three fundamental strategies that can help you gauge your chances of success with any project.

Understanding Client Needs

First, you need to grasp what the client is hiring for. This isn't just about the services you offer; it's about understanding their specific needs. Ask yourself: What value is the client looking to gain? What are they willing to pay for? It's essential to know the types of services, solutions, or approaches they are interested in. For example, if a client is aiming for sustainable design practices, your proposal should reflect this commitment alongside your design skills.

This step lays the foundation for your proposal. If you understand the client's priorities, you can position your offer in a way that makes it resonate with them. When a client sees that you truly understand their needs, they are more likely to view you as a credible and valuable partner.

Identifying the Baggage

Next, it's crucial to consider any "baggage" that might shadow the client's decision-making process. What frustrations or misconceptions do they have about your industry, your firm, or your competitors? These experiences can color their expectations and perceptions, so it's vital to recognize and address them.

For instance, perhaps the client had a bad experience with a previous contractor who over-promised and under-delivered. Acknowledge these kinds of past frustrations in your conversation. Offer transparent communication and show your commitment to meeting their needs. By doing this, you can help mitigate their concerns and build trust.

Finding the Gaps

The third strategy involves understanding what your competition might be lacking. What unique value can you provide that others cannot? This could be a specialized service, an innovative design approach, or exceptional client support. Identifying areas where your competitors falter allows you to set yourself apart.

For example, maybe you offer a unique project management software that streamlines communication and enhances collaboration. Highlight this in your pitch to show how you can save time and reduce stress for the client. By presenting something fresh and valuable, you not only gain attention but also position yourself favorably in the client's mind.

Evaluating Your Competition

Next, you need to assess how well your competition aligns with the three areas we've discussed: understanding client needs, addressing baggage, and offering unique value. If you find that your competition can match or exceed you in these aspects, it might be prudent to reconsider pursuing the project altogether.

Don't chase after every opportunity simply because you need work. A project with a high likelihood of winning is one that aligns with your skills and value proposition. If you believe your chances of winning are lower than 50%, it may not be worth the investment of time and resources.

The Importance of Curiosity

As you move through this assessment process, remain genuinely curious about the client's needs and pain points. Inquire deeply to uncover what they truly value and what their decision-making framework looks like. Open-ended questions can lead to significant insights.

For example, rather than simply asking, "What is your budget?" try asking, "What outcomes are most important to you with this project?" This approach invites conversation and can reveal information that helps you tailor your proposal more effectively. Curiosity can unlock doors that lead you to a better understanding of your chances of success.

Avoiding the Trap of Random Pursuits

In the design business, success is not based on chance. It's a calculated, strategic approach to winning work. Pursuing projects that don't align with your strengths can put your reputation at risk and drain your team's energy and morale.

Focus instead on opportunities that you can pursue with confidence, believing that you have the upper hand. This approach fosters a healthier workplace atmosphere and encourages your team to remain motivated and engaged.

Building a Framework for Success

Developing a methodical framework for assessing project likelihood can guide your decision-making process. Create a checklist of questions and considerations you need to evaluate for each potential project.

This could include:

- What are the client's primary goals?
- What baggage do they carry, and how can you address it?
- What unique value do you offer compared to your competitors?

By categorizing this thinking into a clear framework, you simplify the assessment process, making it easier for you and your team to determine where to invest your efforts.

Conclusion

In summary, assessing your likelihood of winning a particular project requires a thorough understanding of client needs, industry baggage, and competitive advantages. By approaching potential projects with genuine curiosity, you can uncover valuable insights that substantially impact your success.

Remember, it's not about the quantity of work you pursue but the quality of opportunities you choose to chase. Look for projects where your unique offerings shine and walk away from those that don't meet your criteria. This strategic approach will not only improve your chances of winning, but will also ensure your work remains meaningful and impactful.

Chapter Summary:

- **Understand client needs deeply** to tailor your proposals and resonate with their priorities.

- **Acknowledge past frustrations** clients may have; build trust through transparent communication.

- **Identify gaps in competition** and showcase your unique

services to stand out in pitches.

- **Develop a project assessment checklist** to strategically evaluate opportunities and focus efforts.

Chapter Twelve

The Art of Extraction

In the competitive landscape of business development, understanding the motivations and preferences of decision-makers is crucial. This chapter will introduce you to the art of extracting critical unwritten information through a strategic questioning process. By focusing on three essential questions—expressed in two different contexts—you will gain invaluable insights that can propel your career as an emerging design professional, positioning you as an indispensable seller-doer in your field.

The Importance of Insight

First, why is it critical to extract insights from decision-makers? It's about understanding what clients value, their pain points, and their specific needs. This knowledge enables you to tailor your approach, differentiate yourself from competitors, and ultimately secure more work. The right questions can unlock powerful information that informs your strategies and services.

Three Key Questions

Begin by grasping these fundamental questions. These insights won't just offer clarity but bolster your value as a professional. Let's break down the process:

1. What is the one thing the current consultants do so well that they should keep doing?

This question addresses what your client appreciates most about their current providers. As you ask this question, encourage your clients to focus on skills and behaviors rather than specific individuals. When clients articulate what they value, you learn about the qualities that resonate with them. This insight will allow you to position yourself as a consultant who can replicate – or even enhance – those valued traits.

2. What is the one bad habit those consultants have that they need to fix right now?

Here, you are tapping into what might be unsatisfactory about their current experience. This question provides a chance for clients to vent their frustrations constructively. Identifying a bad habit allows you to uncover weaknesses in your competitors' approaches and position yourself as a solution provider. When you openly acknowledge these issues in your discussions, you show a keen understanding of the challenges your clients face.

3. What is the one thing that the current consultants aren't providing, which you wish they would?

This question invites clients to express their unmet needs. By understanding what they believe is lacking in their current relationships, you can highlight how your services can fill those gaps. Clients may feel satisfied yet aware of the additional value they seek. When you deliver on these expectations, you gain a tremendous advantage in fostering long-lasting partnerships.

Different Contexts for the Questions

Now, imagine you are entering a new market or dealing with clients who have little experience hiring design professionals similar to you. Your approach to the three questions remains similar, but with slight modifications to align with the context:

1. What do you think consulting firms need to do every day to provide amazing value?

This helps you uncover general client expectations and desires. New clients may not have specific service providers in mind, so their answers could reveal the very foundation of what they seek in a consultant.

2. What is a bad habit in the consulting industry that you believe we should stop?

This angle allows clients to share their perspectives on the industry. Whether it's slow response times or lack of transparency, understanding their fears gives you insight into the barriers that may prevent them from engaging you.

3. What's a desirable service or approach you wish would simply be included as standard?

This question captures the essence of added value your clients may not even realize they want. With this information, you can either offer it as a complimentary service or as an optional add-on, giving you room to negotiate.

Creating Compelling Value Propositions

When combined, these questions provide a rich tapestry of insights. They enable you to identify your value proposition precisely. By understanding what clients appreciate, what frustrates them, and what they desire, you can craft a compelling offer that is hard to resist.

For instance, using the insights gathered, if a client mentions a particular frustration with their current provider, you could outline how your approach eliminates that problem. Simultaneously, if they express a desire for a certain service, highlight how your offering meets and exceeds those expectations.

The Power of Natural Curiosity

Engage in these interactions with genuine curiosity. This will not only make clients feel valued, but will also enhance your understanding of their needs, solidifying your position as a trusted advisor rather than just another vendor. Ask follow-up questions and seek clarification where needed; this will signal your commitment to truly understanding their situation.

Memorization: Your Edge

As you move forward, memorize these questions. Make them a part of your toolkit. The ability to ask the right questions confidently will give you an edge and build trust with prospects, leading to deeper conversations.

An Invaluable Skill

In conclusion, mastering the art of extraction through focused questioning will empower you in your journey as a design professional. If you consistently ask these questions with genuine curiosity and adeptly follow up for clarity, you'll wield insights that your competition will envy. Building your market share and establishing your credibility will become not just possible, but inevitable. You are, after all, positioning yourself as a valuable partner who understands the intricacies of your clients' needs better than they do.

Chapter Summary:

- Ask decision-makers targeted questions to uncover their genuine needs and preferences.

- Identify current consultants' strengths and weaknesses to differentiate your services.

- Use genuine curiosity to strengthen client relationships and build trust.

- Memorize key questions to enhance your confidence and effectiveness in conversations.

Chapter Thirteen

Building Relationships Beyond Transactions

People often measure success in the world of design and business by numbers and transactions. However, the most successful professionals recognize that their true power lies in relationships. This chapter will guide you on how to build connections that go beyond mere business interactions, establishing a rapport that can elevate your career and enrich your life.

Understanding the Importance of Relationships

First, it's crucial to recognize that the design industry is, at its core, a people's business. If you truly enjoy working with people, you're already on your way to forming valuable connections. Building relationships isn't just about exchanging services or negotiating contracts;

it's about understanding who your clients are, what they value, and how you can genuinely contribute to their success.

Be Interested, Not Interesting

One of the simplest yet most profound pieces of advice comes from a successful entrepreneur I once interviewed: "Be interested, not interesting." Shift your focus from impressing others to genuinely inquiring about them. When you meet potential clients or collaborators, ask questions that matter: "How did you get to this point in your career?" "What challenges are you currently facing?," This approach shows you care, and people naturally gravitate towards those who show genuine interest.

Listening Actively

Listening is a critical skill in building relationships. Active listening means engaging with what the other person is saying, rather than just waiting for your turn to speak. As they share their experiences and challenges, reflect what you hear to ensure understanding. For instance, if a client complains about a project timeline, reaffirm their feelings by saying, "It sounds like meeting the deadline is really important to you." This validates their emotions and fosters trust.

Keep Your Word

Integrity in your commitments is key to relationship building. If you say you will follow up on a request or meet someone at a specific time, be sure to do so. Keeping your promises reinforces your reliability. When clients know they can depend on you, they are more likely to engage with you again, creating a cycle of trust and collaboration.

The Power of Authenticity

Authenticity is the bedrock of meaningful relationships. Clients can sense when someone is being insincere or only trying to achieve a transactional goal. Be open about who you are, including your challenges and insecurities. Sharing experiences that illustrate your vulnerabilities doesn't mean over sharing, but finding common ground that deepens the connection. If you ask about a client's shortcoming, share a related experience of your own first.

Establishing Mutual Respect

Mutual respect is essential for any thriving relationship. As you gradually share personal stories and experiences, it creates a dialogue that can cause a deeper understanding of each other's perspectives. Over time, you both can challenge each other to grow and succeed in the industry, and this synergy makes relationships invaluable.

Vulnerability Builds Connection

Embracing vulnerability can be daunting, yet it forms the cornerstone of genuine connections. By revealing your fears and challenges, you not only allow others to relate to you, but also encourage them to open up in return. We don't build this kind of relationship on superficial small talk; instead, we foster an environment for free exchange and candid discussions.

Understand Different Perspectives

It's important to recognize that not everyone shares the same worldview or values you may hold. Being sensitive and respectful towards differing perspectives is vital. Your ability to engage with someone from a unique background begins with acknowledging their experiences and feelings. As you establish these connections, take care to allow space for open discussions, ensuring everyone feels comfortable sharing.

Emotional Intelligence in Conversations

Emotional intelligence involves understanding the subtext of a conversation. Pay close attention to non-verbal cues such as body language and facial expressions, which can show comfort levels. If you sense someone becoming uneasy, adapt your questions or change the subject. Maintaining the other person's comfort will encourage them to stay engaged and share openly.

Be Genuinely Helpful

Your aim should be to add value to your client's life. As you nurture your relationships, think about ways you can assist them in achieving their goals. This could be through introductions to beneficial contacts or providing insights that could help them overcome specific challenges. These acts of kindness show your sincere concern for their success.

The Long Game: Relationships Over Transactions

Transitioning from a transactional mindset to a relational one can take time and patience. The most successful seller-doers understand that each interaction is an opportunity to strengthen ties. Remember, you are not just selling a service or a product; you are investing in a relationship that could yield long-term benefits for both parties involved.

Shine Through Your Character

As you embark on your journey of relationship building, remember that it's your true character that will shine through in your career. Stay focused on the surrounding people, maintain your integrity, and appreciate the inherent value of those you engage with. Relationships enrich our professional lives, and by nurturing them, you establish a robust foundation for future success. As you grow to see the value of others, you'll also discover new avenues for your own development and opportunities in the business realm. Embrace the journey, and let your authentic self be the guide in building relationships that truly matter.

Chapter Summary:

- Prioritize genuine interest in others to cultivate meaningful connections.

- Listen actively and validate others' feelings for stronger relationships.

- Keep your promises to build trust and reliability with clients.

- Embrace vulnerability and authenticity to deepen professional ties.

Chapter Fourteen

Crafting Proposals That Shine

In the competitive landscape of design and business, a well-crafted proposal can be the key to securing new projects and elevating your career. This chapter will guide you through the essential strategies for creating proposals that stand out and resonate with potential clients. The goal is simple: transform your proposals into powerful tools that communicate your value and expertise clearly and compellingly.

First, let's break down the foundation of a winning proposal. A sound proposal typically includes three major components: a captivating cover letter, a clear and structured approach to the work, and a well-presented team. Think of these elements as the pillars that support your proposal. If any of these areas are weak, the entire structure could crumble.

Start with a Powerful Cover Letter

The cover letter is your first opportunity to make a great impression. It should grab the reader's attention and provide a snapshot of your proposal's value. Picture it as the opening act of a concert — it sets the tone for everything that follows. Start with a hook that directly addresses a pain point or desire of the client. For instance, you might say, "If you're looking to enhance your project outcomes while avoiding common pitfalls, then this could be the most impactful proposal you read this year."

Next, articulate how you plan to deliver value. Clearly state your understanding of the project and the client's needs. This is where you show that you've listened to and truly comprehend their challenges. Then, confidently show that you're ready to jump into action. A line like, "I look forward to discussing how we can start this exciting project together," can leave them eager to learn more.

Highlight Your Unique Approach

Once your cover letter has successfully engaged the client, the next section of your proposal should unpack your unique approach. Highlight what differentiates you from others in your field. This is where your research and insights are vital. If you've identified a specific technique or technology that enhances your efficiency, mention this and explain how it benefits the client. List features, benefits, and the ultimate payoff using bullet points.

For example, if your team has developed a proprietary software that streamlines design processes, outline that software's features concisely. Consider saying,

- Our **innovative software saves up to 20% of project time**, allowing you to bring your vision to reality *faster*.

This clear format helps clients understand the value you offer quickly.

Addressing Client Challenges

Now, turn your attention to the challenges the client is facing. Listing these challenges along with how you plan to resolve them, can be very effective. This could look something like: "Some of the major concerns include tight deadlines and budget constraints. We will tackle these by implementing our proven project management framework that has consistently delivered projects on time and within budget."

Remember, when making a claim about your capabilities, be ready to back it up with evidence. This could be as case studies, testimonials, or specific successes in past projects. The more you prove your credibility, the more confidence the client will have in your proposal.

Showcase Your Team's Expertise

The next critical element is showcasing your team. Here, you want to emphasize that you have the right mix of skills and personality to tackle the project effectively. Highlight the accomplishments of specific team members rather than assigning general skills to the entire team. For example, you might write: "Meet Sarah, our industry-leading architect with over a decade of experience designing sustainable buildings."

Providing quick biographical sketches of your team members shows that you've put thought into assembling a qualified team tailored to the project's needs and the client's temperament. It's also helpful to highlight previous collaborations and successful projects to illustrate your team's capability.

Structuring the Proposal

For the structure of your proposal, consider following the order of the client's selection criteria. This makes it easy for them to navigate and see how you meet their priorities. For example, if they listed approach, timeline, and past experience as their top concerns, address these in that order within your proposal. At each juncture, refer back to the sections of the proposal that further elaborate on your claims.

This layout not only helps in clarity but also encourages the client to keep reading and engage with your proposal. You might say, "For a deeper look at how we meet your timeline requirements, please refer to page 15."

The Importance of an Engaging Narrative

Crafting your proposal as a narrative can make it more engaging. Use storytelling techniques to convey your approach and the challenges you've faced. A narrative paints a picture for the client and makes your proposal memorable. For example, share a short story about a project where you learned from a past mistake and developed a highly effective solution. This creates a personal touch that resonates with potential clients.

Concluding Your Proposal Strongly

Conclude your proposal with a strong call to action. This can be as straightforward as, "We're excited about the possibility of working together and would love to set up a meeting to discuss next steps." Make it as easy as possible for them to reach out to you for further discussions. Including your contact information ensures they have everything they need to move forward.

Final Thoughts on Developing Winning Proposals

By now, you should have the tools to craft proposals that shine. Keep practicing these techniques and refining your approach. Remember, you've already done the hard work of making your proposal unique by laying out the groundwork beforehand. You understood the client's needs and created tailored solutions.

Ultimately, great proposals don't just happen; they stem from thoughtfulness, preparation, and an understanding of the client's world. With dedication and the right strategies, your proposals can rise above the competition and show your clients the invaluable asset you truly are. So, roll up those sleeves and let your unique proposals pave the way to your success!

Chapter Summary:

- Start with a powerful cover letter that addresses client needs and sets the tone.

- Highlight your unique approach with logical benefits and evidence of your capabilities.

- Showcase your team's expertise with specific bios and examples of past successes.

- Structure your proposal to align with client priorities and conclude with a strong call to action.

Chapter Fifteen

The Power of Storytelling in Business Development

In the world of business development, especially for design professionals, storytelling holds a profound and transformative power. While many may view proposals and interviews as dry, technical processes, this chapter intends to reveal how weaving a narrative can tilt the scales in your favor. Through effective storytelling, you can not only resonate with your audience but also position yourself as an indispensable part of their project.

Engagement and authenticity lie at the heart of storytelling. When you craft a proposal, think of your cover letter as your opening act. This is where you will first capture your reader's attention. Instead of launching straight into technical jargon or bureaucratic detail, articulate your understanding of the client's needs and frame it in a compelling narrative. If you can capture their attention with a relatable opening and a confident assertion of your ability to deliver value, you'll establish a foundation for a successful interaction.

For example, begin your cover letter with an intriguing hook. Consider a line like, "If you're looking for innovative solutions that will elevate your project while steering clear of common pitfalls, you have found the right team." Such a statement shows your understanding of both the challenges they face and the avenues for growth. Remember, storytelling is about connection. You want the client to feel that you not only understand their situation, but are excited about the possibility of working together.

Next, go beyond mere acknowledgment of their challenges. Dive deeper into the storytelling aspect by showcasing how your unique approach distinguishes you from the competition. Reference proprietary technology, a specialized team, or innovative strategies that you alone are offering. For instance, you might say, "Our team has developed a proprietary system that streamlines project management, allowing for real-time adjustments and ultimately delivering higher quality results." By using storytelling to highlight your unique selling points, you give the client an obvious reason to choose your proposal over others.

Using bullet points can also be an effective storytelling tool in your proposal. List the client's selection criteria as bullet points, and follow each with a brief explanation that illustrates both the feature and its benefit. For example, "Feature: Dedicated project manager; Benefit: Ensures streamlined communication and rapid problem-solving." This structure allows your storytelling to appear organized and digestible, reinforcing your ability to deliver results.

As you elaborate on your approach, frame your narrative around addressing their most pressing challenges. Think of challenges in terms of people, processes, places, and things. Share stories of prior successes where you have navigated similar obstacles, demonstrating how your experience has equipped you to tackle the current project. Concrete examples, drawn from your history, will not only substantiate your claims but make them relatable to the client.

Every claim you make should hearken back to specific experiences. If you state that your methodology is tried and true, provide a brief narrative about a past project where this was clear. Avoid vague proclamations. Instead, say something like, "In our last large-scale project, we faced challenges similar to yours, which we overcame through careful planning and team collaboration." Such clarity not only enhances your credibility but also shows that you've learned from experience.

For assembling your team, storytelling still plays a role. Avoid the temptation to present your colleagues as mere names and titles. Instead, introduce them with stories that illustrate their expertise and value. For example, you might say, "John, our lead architect, has not only overseen many successful projects but also pioneered construction techniques that have significantly improved client satisfaction." By creating personal connections, you enhance the client's trust in your team.

The format of your approach shouldn't feel stiff or out of touch. Rather, if you approach it as if you were speaking directly to the client over coffee, your language will be conversational and relatable. This fresh take can help in crafting proposals that feel authentic and personal. After all, clients want to work with people, not just firms. When you write as if you're having a natural conversation, your storytelling flows more readily and connects with readers on a deeper level.

Your project is, ultimately, a narrative waiting to be told. Think of every proposal, every interview, and every pitch as a chapter in that story. By understanding the client's needs and articulating how your work connects with their goals, you build a compelling case for them to choose you. This approach creates a shared narrative that invites them into a partnership, rather than treating them strictly as a buyer of services.

In conclusion, storytelling is not only beneficial but essential in business development. It allows you to craft narratives that convey your understandings, demonstrate value, and illustrate how you can solve problems. As a design professional, the ability to tell stories effectively in your proposals and interviews can elevate your status from a mere provider to an invaluable collaborator. Engage your audience, evoke emotions, and most importantly, humanize your offerings. Remember, storytelling is the key to victory. Embrace it, refine it, and let it guide you towards becoming an unstoppable force in your business development journey.

Chapter Summary:

- Begin proposals with compelling stories to capture attention and connect with clients.

- Showcase your unique approach through narratives that highlight your differentiators.

- Use bullet points to explain client needs, emphasizing features and benefits clearly.

- Treat every communication as a story, inviting clients to see the value of collaboration.

Chapter Sixteen

Communicate to Connect

Effective communication is the lifeblood of successful business development. For design professionals stepping into the realm of client engagement, understanding how to convey ideas and connect with clients is crucial. Many of us have honed our technical skills through rigorous education and practice; however, communication—particularly in a business context—is often neglected. Just like mastering a new design tool or software, mastering communication is vital for anyone who wishes to take charge of their workload and be recognized as a valuable seller-doer in their field.

In the early stages of your career, you may realize that traditional education focuses largely on analytical skills—math, science, and technical proficiency. The world is painted in black and white, where there's always a concrete answer. However, successful client engagement requires a paradigm shift. It hinges on emotional intelligence, active listening, and the ability to articulate ideas clearly and persuasively. This chapter will guide you step by step in developing these essential soft skills.

Step 1: Understand the Importance of Communication

Before delving into actionable tips, it's important to grasp why effective communication matters in your role. Clients want to feel confident that you understand their needs and can deliver solutions that meet and exceed their expectations. When you connect with clients through effective communication, you foster trust and rapport, which are essential for long-term partnerships and successful projects. Remember, the outcome of a project isn't solely determined by technical skills; it's also influenced by how well you communicate your ideas.

Step 2: Build Your Framework

To become effective in your communication, you need a well-defined framework. Think of this framework as a set of guiding principles that dictate how you approach client interactions. Start by documenting what you've learned through experience. This could be a simple outline of your thoughts and strategies. By doing so, you provide your team with tools to grow and succeed alongside you.

Step 3: Harness Visual Communication

You need not be a graphic artist to use visual aids effectively. A picture can convey complex ideas quickly and clearly, so use visuals to enhance your communication. Familiarize yourself with tools that help create simple graphics and charts, which can illustrate your points during presentations or proposals. For instance, if you're discussing a design concept, create a professional-looking sketch or diagram. This can significantly simplify your explanation and help the client visualize your ideas better.

Step 4: Craft Your Written Communication

In written communication, clarity is key. Avoid using passive voice and convoluted sentences. Use concise, active language. Leverage digital tools that can help refine your writing. These tools often highlight areas needing improvement and suggest corrections. For example, if you're drafting a project proposal, focus on clear headings, bullet points, and a straightforward structure. This improves readability and ensures your key points stand out.

Step 5: Develop Public Speaking Skills

Public speaking can intimidate, but practice makes perfect. Take every opportunity to speak in front of others, even if you're uncomfortable. This could be as simple as sharing ideas during team meetings or presenting project updates. Visualize the audience as one person sitting in front of you; this makes the experience less daunting. Over time, as you become more comfortable speaking, your ability to engage clients during interviews or presentations will naturally improve.

Step 6: Engage with Confidence During Interviews

While presenting to clients, focus your communication on the decision-makers in the room. Establishing rapport is essential; it requires active engagement. Listen carefully to their questions and respond thoughtfully. This fosters a collaborative atmosphere, making it easier to address concerns and clarify intentions.

Step 7: Master Negotiation Skills

Negotiation is an integral part of business development and is a dialogue focused on mutual benefits. Effective negotiations revolve around understanding and accommodating each party's perspective. Books and resources on negotiation tactics can enhance your skills, but the most critical tool at your disposal is active listening. Active listening allows you to better understand your client's needs and concerns, equipping you to propose solutions that satisfy both parties.

Step 8: Recognize When to Walk Away

Learning to value your time and expertise is crucial. If a negotiation does not lead to a fair outcome, sometimes it's best to walk away. Not every opportunity will align with your values or the quality of work you wish to deliver. Reflect on the experience and identify valuable lessons you can apply moving forward.

The Key Takeaway

Communication skills may not have been a focus in your formal education, but they are just as critical as any technical skill you have gained. The ability to communicate effectively will set you apart as a seller-doer and empower you to take control of your professional journey. As you cultivate these skills, remember that every interaction is an opportunity for connection and collaboration. By investing in your communication abilities, you are not just improving your career prospects; you are building the foundation for lasting client relationships and meaningful work experiences.

Chapter Summary:

- Recognize that effective communication fosters trust and long-term client relationships.

- Establish a framework to document and improve your communication strategies.

- Use visuals to simplify complex ideas and enhance client presentations.

- Practice public speaking and negotiation skills to engage more confidently with clients.

Chapter Seventeen

Avoiding Pitfalls in the Sales Cycle

In the fast-paced world of design, successfully navigating the sales cycle is crucial for upcoming design professionals who want to become indispensable seller-doers. However, many designers stumble into common pitfalls that hinder their progress and diminish their effectiveness. This chapter will help you recognize these pitfalls and provide you with strategies to avoid them, ultimately saving you time, money, and frustration.

Understanding the Reactionary Mode

One of the most significant blunders design professionals make is entering the proposal process reactively. This often happens when the pressure is on - perhaps project demands increase, or finances become tight. In desperate times, it's easy to chase after every project, even those for which you're not adequately prepared. This desperate approach can undermine your proposals and diminish your team's morale.

When you're scrambling to respond to every opportunity, the quality of your work can suffer. You're likely to put together a mediocre proposal, which not only reflects poorly on you but can also impact how your team feels. No one enjoys "going all in" on a project that has a low chance of success, and repeating this cycle can lead to burnout. Instead, cultivating a proactive mindset is key to success in the sales cycle.

The Power of Pre-Positioning

To break free from the reactionary mindset, focus on a strategy called pre-positioning. Pre-positioning means preparing yourself and your team before a project officially hits the market. This helps you better understand the client's needs and how your skills uniquely position you to provide value. This proactive approach allows you to build relationships and gather insights that others might miss.

Asking three simple questions upfront can lead to a deeper understanding of both the potential client and your own team. These questions should focus on:

1. What are the specific needs and goals of the client?
2. How can our team best address these needs?
3. What challenges might arise during this project, and how can we mitigate them?

These questions enable you to gather valuable information to inform your proposal and position your team as a trusted partner right from the start.

Gathering Preliminary Information

Understanding the technical aspects of a project is an essential part of pre-positioning. Before jumping into a project, try gathering preliminary information. Schedule a brainstorming session with your team to discuss not only the proposed work, but also how to tackle it effectively. Explore the intricacies of the project and work collectively to draft an initial understanding of what needs to happen.

This step may involve diving into research, connecting with industry experts, or even reaching out to the client for clarification. Having a clear grasp of the project requirements allows you to build a solid proposal based on informed insights rather than assumptions.

Building the Right Team

An effective proposal doesn't happen in isolation; it's a collaborative effort. Assembling the right team is a critical component of pre-positioning. By identifying who will be involved in delivering the project, you can effectively expect the complexity of the tasks ahead. Your team should include not only design professionals but also specialists who add value to other areas.

Engage in discussions with your sub-consultants and partners to garner their insights and expertise. This collective approach ensures that you deliver a holistic proposal that addresses the client's needs from multiple angles, setting your work apart from the competition.

Engaging with the Client

Establishing a thorough line of communication with your potential client is vital. Open dialogue allows you to ask follow-up questions that can clarify any uncertainties, and it can reveal critical information that shapes your proposal. You should aim to educate the client on any challenges they might not have previously considered, addressing how your unique strengths lay a path toward effective solutions.

Being proactive in your communication shows your commitment and positions you as a knowledgeable partner throughout the process. The more insight you gather, the better your proposal can be tailored to the client's needs.

Understanding the Competition

A successful proposal doesn't just rest on your team's strengths; it's also essential to know who you're up against. Researching your competition gives you insights into their strengths and weaknesses. Usually, competitors will have specific technical capabilities, diverse work portfolios, or unique approaches worth studying.

Taking the time to analyze where competitors excel or fall short allows you to differentiate your proposal effectively. Collaborate with your team to devise strategies for outperforming the competition. Explore creative solutions, efficient project delivery, and distinctive project approaches. This insight adds a competitive layer, positioning your work more favorably in the client's eyes.

Resource Management

As you consider pre-positioning strategies, remember that you have limited resources like time, energy, and finances. Continuing to pursue projects without thoughtful preparation squanders these valuable resources, diverting them from more fruitful endeavors, such as securing other opportunities or building stronger relationships.

Minimizing wasted efforts not only results in better business decisions. By honing in on well-researched opportunities, you create a ripple effect: increased win rates, improved morale, and ultimately, more vibrant business development efforts.

Steering Away from Burnout

Through proactive pre-positioning, you can effectively combat the cycle of burnout that often accompanies a reactionary sales process. By being strategic and aligning your team's efforts, you cultivate a healthy work environment that values collaboration and thoughtful engagement, rather than frantic last-minute submissions.

Your commitment to well-positioning your team not only makes for stronger proposals but also fosters a company culture that is sustainable, focusing on quality over quantity.

Becoming a Lean, Agile Organization

Ultimately, knowing about an opportunity before it actually hits the market is the most critical element in avoiding pitfalls in the sales cycle. By developing a culture of pre-positioning, your organization can grow leaner and more agile in its approach. You'll be prepared to seize opportunities with confidence, leveraging your unique advantages and rich insights into clients and competition.

The Road Ahead

In conclusion, as you embark on your journey through the sales cycle, be mindful of these pitfalls and the importance of pre-positioning. By prioritizing preparation over reaction, engaging your team, and fostering open communication with clients, you can set yourself on a path toward success. Recognizing what it takes to be seen as a valuable seller-doer will not only improve your proposal outcomes, but also enable you to forge lasting relationships with clients and partners. Embrace this proactive mindset, and you'll find that the sales cycle can transform from a series of challenges into a dynamic opportunity for growth.

Chapter Summary:

- Shift from reactive to proactive in your approach to sales proposals.

- Ask key questions to understand client needs and team capabilities.

- Build a collaborative team to enhance proposal quality and effectiveness.

- Develop open communication with clients to tailor solutions and avoid burnout.

Chapter Eighteen

The Lifelong Value of Follow-Ups in Client Relations

Building and maintaining client relationships is essential in the world of design and professional services. You might think that winning a proposal is the end of the road, but in reality, it's just the beginning of a much longer journey. Establishing solid follow-up practices after you've secured a project can transform you from a onetime service provider into a trusted partner. Let's explore why follow-ups are essential and how they can significantly impact your success.

To understand the value of follow-ups, let's consider the scenario of winning a project. Congratulations, you've landed the job! However, the critical work is only starting. This is where your follow-up strategy becomes indispensable. Following a successful proposal, it is vital to immediately reconnect with the client. A simple "How are we doing?" You can begin an ongoing dialogue by asking "How are we doing?", which can uncover any hidden concerns or expectations that may not have been addressed during the initial discussions.

One of the biggest hurdles in client relations is the disconnect that can occur between different teams. While the production team may feel one way about project progress, the client might have a different narrative. You must be the bridge that connects these perspectives. By frequently checking in, you can ensure that everyone is on the same page, which helps to build trust and makes your role as a seller-doer even more invaluable.

Let's talk figures: a staggering 80% of business in a successful professional services firm should come from repeat clients. This statistic highlights that maintaining relationships is not just a supporting act, but a starring role in your career. Finding new clients can be incredibly expensive and time-consuming. In contrast, nurturing existing relationships through thoughtful follow-ups is often much quicker and less costly. Your goal should be to become the go-to person for current clients, making them rely on your expertise and creativity.

After signing the contract, a check-in call is the perfect next step. This conversation establishes where everyone stands after the business development process, including the proposal and negotiations. Building upon this momentum can reveal additional opportunities for collaboration or adjustments in expectations. It also sets the stage for outlining communication styles, frequency of updates, and meeting norms, all of which are crucial as the project unfolds.

Throughout the lifecycle of a project, maintaining regular touchpoints is critical. As the project progresses, ensure that the narratives you hear from your team align with your client's feedback. This consistent monitoring prevents misunderstandings and logistical issues from arising as you manage deliverables, invoicing, or any technology hiccups.

Another key aspect we must consider is team stability on both sides. Changes in team members can introduce a level of unpredictability. Whether it's because of promotions, new hires, or departures, these transitions can disrupt the continuity of service. When a leader or key team member leaves, it's essential to communicate this change transparently with the client. You don't want them to feel like they are experiencing a bait-and-switch scenario, where the skills and personality that earned you the job seem to disappear overnight.

Whenever a change occurs, document what made the original team special. This could include shared understanding, specific processes followed, or simply the chemistry built. If the new team cannot replicate the magic of the initial relationship, it may be time to renegotiate what the client can expect. Being upfront about potential shifts shows professionalism and strengthens your credibility.

As your project draws to a close, it's vital to conduct a reflective review with your client. How well did the project meet their expectations? Did your team deliver? This debriefing will not only help you understand areas for improvement but also position you for future opportunities. Outlining the next steps clearly can guide the project evolution and illustrate your proactive approach.

Start a real-world conversation about what the client needs next. Use your insights from the completed project to propose opportunities where you can add value. If your interaction was positive, the client might already be eager to work with you again.

In summary, the value of follow-ups in client relations extends far beyond the immediate project at hand. They are the lifeblood of lasting relationships that yield continuous business opportunities. Without follow-up, your words may become hollow, lacking the substance needed to forge strong connections.

So, remember, establishing these follow-up practices not only enhances your credibility but creates a framework for sustained collaboration. By embracing a culture of communication and attention to detail, you can ensure that clients feel valued, understood, and eager to return with future projects. Your role as a seller-doer will flourish, marked by empowered client relationships that contribute meaningfully to your ongoing success.

Chapter Summary:

- Start follow-ups immediately after winning a project to maintain open communication.

- Regularly check in with clients to bridge any narrative gaps between teams.

- Document key team strengths to manage changes and maintain client trust effectively.

- Conduct reflective reviews at project close to identify improvements and future opportunities.

Chapter Nineteen

Measuring Success in Business Development

As an emerging design professional, entering the business development arena might seem daunting. However, measuring your success doesn't have to be complex. In this chapter, we'll unpack straightforward metrics and indicators that can provide you with a clear picture of how you're doing in your efforts to grow your client base and enhance your reputation as a valuable seller-doer.

Understanding Key Metrics

First on our journey is the **hit rate**—a fundamental indicator in any sales game. Think of it as your scoreboard. Your hit rate is calculated by comparing the number of projects you win to the total number of opportunities you pursue. For instance, if you chase 10 projects and win 3, your hit rate is 30%. This simple number can reveal whether you're effectively connecting with the right opportunities or if you need to refine your approach.

Next, let's consider the **no-go rate**. This metric tracks your ability to identify which opportunities to pursue and which ones to pass on. It reflects your strategic thinking and discernment. If you find that many opportunities you pass on disappear without any pursuit, it might show that you're missing out on valuable prospects or not qualifying opportunities as well as you should. A keen understanding of what makes up an excellent opportunity will sharpen your overall business development skills.

As you build your pipeline of work, it's critical to monitor the **size of your funnel**—or the total number of opportunities you are tracking. Here's a handy rule of thumb: chase ten times the amount of work you need to sustain your business. Why ten times? Simple: many opportunities often do not materialize, your hit-rate won't be 100%, and some wins won't materials due to funding or bad contract terms. For example, if you need to earn $100,000 to keep your team afloat, aim for $1,000,000 in potential projects. This approach accommodates the inevitable drop-offs in projects along the way and allows for a more stable workload.

Keeping Track of Client Satisfaction

A seamless connection between client satisfaction and your success cannot be overstated. Repeat business is not only a sign of a job well done but also a testament to the relationships you're building with clients. Measuring the percentage of your work that comes from returning clients can help you gauge how well you meet client expectations. The higher that percentage, the better your reputation grows, leading to even more business opportunities.

To dig even deeper into your business strategy, ask yourself how you can increase repeat business. Evaluate client feedback after project completion. Understand their pain points and expect their future needs. Satisfied clients often refer you to new prospects, expanding your network and enhancing your reputation.

The Cost of Winning Work

Moving on, it's essential to track the **cost of acquiring new clients**. Business development isn't free; there's a tangible investment in time and resources. Document everything you spend on marketing, proposal writing, client meetings, and even attending trade shows. By accumulating this data, you can calculate it as a percentage of the total project value—let's call it your "cost of winning."

For example, if you spend $10,000 pursuing a project worth $100,000, your cost of winning is 10%. Knowing this number helps you evaluate whether chasing certain opportunities is worth the investment. The more efficient you become in this process, the better your profit margins will be once you secure that work.

Identifying Successful Patterns

You might also want to examine the **common attributes** of the projects you successfully win. This could include factors like the type of project, geographical location, or a particular client. Analyzing these patterns can arm you with the insights you need to target similar opportunities in the future or to identify where you may need to innovate.

For instance, if you find that most of your successful projects have been in a specific sector, consider focusing your business development efforts in that direction. As you hire new talent and expand your offerings, this insight can guide how you allocate resources effectively.

Building a Simple System

As we wrap up this chapter, let's return to our core purpose: developing a simple and effective system to measure your success. Start small. Track your hit and no-go rates, client satisfaction, pipeline size, costs, and attributes of winning projects. By systematically recording these figures, you create a robust overview of your business development success.

Remember, **things that don't get tracked don't improve**. Keeping your finger on the pulse of these metrics allows you to make informed decisions. Are you spending your time and money wisely? Are you on the right path to grow your pipeline? Reflecting on these questions will steer your efforts toward profitability and maintain a positive morale within your team.

Chapter Summary:

- Track your hit rate: evaluate project wins versus opportunities to refine your approach.

- Understand your no-go rate: improve strategic thinking by assessing pursued opportunities wisely.

- Monitor client satisfaction: increase repeat business by gathering feedback and addressing client needs.

- Calculate costs of winning: ensure your business development efforts yield profitable results.

Chapter Twenty

Collaboration as a Catalyst for Enhanced Sales Efforts

In the competitive landscape of design and engineering firms, collaboration is often the quiet powerhouse driving success. For up-and-coming design professionals, understanding how to work effectively with your colleagues across different teams can significantly enhance your sales efforts. This chapter will explore the vital role of collaboration and how it can transform your approach to business development, making you not just a seller-but an invaluable seller-doer.

Understanding the Power of Teamwork

Imagine a bustling orchestra. Each musician plays a different instrument, yet they come together to create beautiful music. Similarly, in a firm, diverse teams—sales, production, operations, human resources, and executive leadership—must harmonize to create a seamless workflow. When these teams communicate openly and effectively, they foster an environment where ideas and resources flow, ultimately enhancing sales capabilities.

Open Lines of Communication

First, it's crucial to establish open lines of communication. This means ensuring that sales teams meet regularly with production teams to discuss current and upcoming projects. What's the status of a project? Are there any delays? Understanding these details helps sales professionals set realistic expectations for clients and offers insights into potential upselling opportunities.

Incorporate regular catchups where teams share updates and challenges. Picture this: You're in a sales meeting discussing client needs when a member of the operations team casually mentions a new capability or resource that just became available. That's information that could lead to closing a deal!

Aligning with Executive Vision

Next, understanding your firm's executive direction is essential. It's not enough to know that your company has a strategic plan; you need to grasp its nuances. By collaborating with executives, you learn about the vision and priorities guiding the business. This knowledge allows you to tailor your sales approach and align it with the company's goals.

For instance, suppose the executives have determined that sustainability is a key focus area for the coming year. If sales teams are aware of this direction, they can emphasize sustainable practices in proposals, showcasing the firm as forward-thinking and invested in current trends.

Leveraging Operational Expertise

Collaboration with the operations team offers another layer of understanding. Their knowledge about labor, equipment, and logistics significantly contributes to crafting accurate proposals. For instance, if you have a well-established relationship with operations, you can quickly determine if a project is workable and what resources are available.

Imagine preparing a proposal for a large-scale design project, but you only discover during negotiations that the team won't be available for six months. By regularly communicating with operations, you could avoid that embarrassing scenario entirely and present your clients with realistic timelines.

Understanding Human Resources Challenges

Equally important is the role of human resources in this collaborative ecosystem. Human resources teams can share critical insights about staff capabilities, challenges, and even morale. By understanding the challenges faced by staff, human resources can inform how projects are pitched to clients.

For example, if human resources shares that many employees are overworked and morale is low, your team may decide to adjust project scopes or timelines to relieve pressure—ultimately leading to higher quality work and happier employees.

Cultivating Company Culture

Company culture is another crucial aspect to consider. Culture affects everything, from performance to employee satisfaction. When everyone is on the same page regarding company values and culture, your team can create proposals that resonate with potential clients.

Think about a firm that prides itself on collaboration and innovation. By understanding these cultural pillars, sales professionals can highlight these qualities in proposals, differentiating your firm in a crowded market.

Integration for Success

Integrating various teams isn't just about conversation; it's about action. At many firms, people are balancing multiple roles, not just sales or design work. By knowing colleagues' workloads and specialties, you can effectively assemble the best team for a proposal or project.

For instance, if a project requires specific expertise not found within your team, understanding who excels in those areas allows you to bring in the right sub-consultants. This strategic alliance highlights the breadth of your firm's capabilities and enhances your value in the eyes of potential clients.

Learning from Each Other

Collaboration opens the door to invaluable lessons from both victories and failures. By discussing experiences in team meetings, you learn what strategies worked and which ones didn't. Perhaps a previous proposal failed because it underestimated a project's complexity. By sharing such insights, you enable the entire team to grow and improve its approach.

Collect tales of both success and setbacks. These lessons become a repository of knowledge that can enhance future projects and proposals, giving everyone more tools in their toolbox for client engagement.

Embracing Change and Trends

In the design and engineering fields, trends and market dynamics are ever-changing. Collaboration ensures that your team stays informed about market adjustments, new technologies, and shifting client expectations. Regularly touching base with different teams helps your firm adapt its strategies based on real-time feedback from various angles of the business.

Hold idea sessions to share what's trending in your industry. These gatherings can inspire innovative proposals or client engagement tactics that people might not have thought of otherwise.

Capitalizing on Resources

At the end of the day, understanding the resources available within your firm can make all the difference. Whether it's tools, personnel, or knowledge, knowing what you can tap into is vital. Regular collaboration with different teams allows you to use strengths and fill gaps in capabilities.

As you pursue additional work, always check with your team to see what can be shared. For example, if you need a visual aesthetic for a proposal, your marketing team may have relevant graphics or insights into what resonates with prospective clients.

Together, We Achieve More

In conclusion, remember that sales and business development are not the solo endeavors they often seem. Collaboration amplifies your efforts by fostering a shared understanding of goals, resources, and challenges. When teams work together—sharing knowledge and supporting one another—you don't just enhance your sales efforts; you create a resilient and adaptable organization.

Each interaction with your colleagues provides opportunities to learn, adapt, and improve. More ideas, more relationships, and more collaboration will always lead to better outcomes. You're not just contributing to your role—you're becoming a crucial part of a well-oiled machine dedicated to delivering exceptional work for your clients. So, embrace collaboration as the catalyst it is, and watch your sales efforts flourish!

Chapter Summary:

- Foster open communication with team members for better project insights and sales success.

- Align your sales strategies with company goals to emphasize key focus areas.

- Cultivate relationships across teams to leverage expertise and streamline proposal development.

- Share lessons from past projects to enhance team growth and improve future proposals.

Chapter Twenty-One

Balancing Act

As an emerging design professional, you're likely passionate about your technical work. However, to maximize your career potential and become an invaluable asset to your organization, it's crucial to balance your technical skills with business acumen. This chapter aims to guide you on this balancing act, where spending just a little time each week on business development can make a significant impact on your professional growth. Let's explore how you can achieve this equilibrium and thrive as a seller-doer in your industry.

Step 1: Join Professional Organizations

Start your journey by engaging with professional organizations related to your field. These organizations are treasure troves of information and networking opportunities. By attending events and meetings where your clients and other professionals congregate, you can gain insight into their needs and challenges. Think of it like stepping outside your immediate circle—the production team, project managers, and discipline leaders—to discover the larger landscape of your industry.

Step 2: Learn About Client Needs

When you're networking, pay attention to the conversations around you. What problems are clients trying to solve? What solutions are other professionals exploring? This outside perspective is invaluable. By understanding client needs better, you'll position yourself to identify how your technical skills align with potential projects or challenges they face. For instance, if you hear clients struggle with sustainable design or new regulations, you could highlight your experience and solutions in that area.

Step 3: Engage with Your Team

Once you gather insights, bring that knowledge back to your team. Engage in conversations about current projects and discuss what you've learned from your networking efforts. By collaborating, you can spark new ideas and reveal potential avenues for business development that may have been overlooked. Your colleagues will also appreciate your willingness to contribute, which helps cultivate a culture of teamwork.

Step 4: Embrace Active Listening

Active listening is a skill that can unlock many doors in business development. When conversing with clients or colleagues, focus on understanding their perspectives. Ask questions that dive deeper into their needs and concerns. This engagement not only demonstrates your commitment but also allows you to bring back relevant information to your team. Through active listening, you'll uncover opportunities and solutions that can lead to project wins.

Step 5: Conduct Research

Dedicate some of your personal time to research industry trends and potential opportunities. This doesn't need to be a time-consuming endeavor; even a few hours each week can make a difference. Use online resources, industry reports, and social media to stay informed about emerging challenges your clients might face. Building a habit of regular research will enhance your knowledge base and make you a go-to resource for your team.

Step 6: Take Part in Proposal Reviews

One effective way to gain insight into the business side of your organization is by participating in proposal reviews. Ask your management if you can participate in proposal reviews, even as an observer. This experience will help you understand how your organization presents itself to clients and the strategies that are at play. Observing this process can provide you with tools and knowledge you can apply to your own projects in the future.

Step 7: Get Involved in Client Interviews

Don't shy away from opportunities to take part in client interviews. These interactions are valuable for understanding client expectations and preferences. Even if you're not in a speaking role, being present during these discussions allows you to absorb important information about the client's decision-making process. Being involved can also reinforce to clients that your organization values developing future talent.

Step 8: Find Small Injection Points

As you balance your time between technical work and business development, look for small injection points during your day. These might include setting aside 30 minutes for networking or dedicating time weekly to read industry articles. Over time, these small commitments add up and contribute significantly to your business acumen development.

Step 9: Collaborate and Share Insights

Regularly share your findings and insights with your colleagues. A collaborative environment benefits everyone and encourages knowledge sharing across the organization. By holding sessions where you present the opportunities you identified or trends you've uncovered, you reinforce your role as a valuable asset in the business development cycle.

Step 10: Measure Your Progress

As you embark on this journey, examine your personal progress. Are you more engaged in business conversations at work? Have clients recognized your contributions? Keep track of these developments, as they serve as motivation to continue balancing your technical responsibilities with business acumen development.

Step 11: Dedicate Time Religiously

Finally, make a commitment to this balance and dedicate time to it religiously. Whether it's daily, weekly, or monthly, having a set schedule will ensure that you're not just a hobbyist—someone with a fleeting interest—but a successful business developer actively contributing to your organization's success.

Chapter Summary:

- Join professional organizations to network and understand broader industry needs.

- Engage actively with your team to spark business development ideas.

- Dedicate time for research and client interactions to enhance your market insights.

- Measure your progress and commit to regular business development efforts.

Chapter Twenty-Two

Showcasing Seller-Doer Value

In today's competitive market, the role of design professionals is evolving. Not only are clients looking for innovative designs, but they also want to work with professionals who can contribute meaningfully to the business development and sales cycle. Becoming a seller-doer allows you to take control of your workload and establish yourself as an invaluable asset to your company. In this chapter, we will explore practical strategies you can implement to showcase your value as a seller-doer.

Bringing Value through Participation

One of the most straightforward ways to show your value is by participating actively in meetings and discussions. When you join project team meetings, focus your attention on the insights shared by your colleagues. Listening carefully to comments about the work being done—whether it involves design, execution, or client relations—can provide you with valuable information that you can leverage to drive better outcomes.

Engaging meaningfully not only strengthens your understanding of the project but also shows to your team and clients that you are committed to success. Remember, showing genuine interest lays the groundwork for a deeper professional relationship.

Take Initiative with Ideas

Don't just sit back and observe; offer your ideas and suggestions. If you believe that a certain strategy or resource could elevate your project, articulate it in team settings. For instance, if you have a fresh approach to a design challenge or a novel idea for client engagement, share it! This proactive attitude showcases your commitment to improvement and your capability as a valuable team member.

Get Your Hands Dirty

Being a seller-doer means rolling up your sleeves and diving into the work. Offer to take on tasks that might initially seem outside your usual responsibilities. Perhaps you could volunteer to draft a proposal or create graphics for a presentation. Even if those responsibilities are tangential to your primary role, stepping outside your comfort zone is a great way to ease the workload of others and build your skills.

Firsthand involvement in diverse tasks positions you not only as a reliable teammate but also as someone who can contribute to the client's experience more holistically.

Show Genuine Interest in Client Success

When attending professional events or client meetings, ask the right questions. This not only shows your keen interest in the client's success, but also reinforces the idea that the entire team is invested. Whether it's discussing challenges they've faced in the past or their vision for future projects, showing that you listen and care about ensuring their success will set you apart.

Being attentive during discussions provides insight into how you can tailor your services to better meet their needs and how you can position yourself as a trusted partner in their business journey.

Collaboration on Proposals

Many times, securing new projects involves drafting proposals. Rather than leaving this task solely to the sales team, become involved. Contribute by providing insights from your project experience to make the proposal more comprehensive. When the client sees that the same professionals working on their projects are also behind their proposals, it reinforces trust and credibility.

This collaborative approach not only showcases your commitment to the project but also gives weight to your perspective as a contributor, which is essential in building long-term relationships.

Deliver High-Quality Work

At the core of showcasing your value as a seller-doer is the quality of your work. Strive to exceed expectations by delivering high-quality outputs. This means ensuring your work is technically correct, free of errors, and delivered on time. The fewer change orders and requests for information (RFIs) you have on a project, the more it reflects your strong communication skills and ability to meet the project requirements.

Taking ownership of your work is critical. Before submitting it for review, conduct a thorough quality check. This habit not only improves the team's work but also builds your reputation as someone who can be relied on for excellence and dependability.

Building Relationships

As you consistently contribute valuable insights and deliver exceptional work, begin building relationships with clients and stakeholders. Genuine connections can cause more opportunities for collaborative projects or referrals. Maintain open lines of communication, providing clients with updates and soliciting feedback. By consistently communicating with stakeholders, you can keep them informed and demonstrate your commitment to their satisfaction.

Positioning Yourself As an Authority

As you gain experience and establish a reputation for being both a doer and a seller, you will position yourself as an authority in your field. This authority will allow you to command higher rates for your work, reflecting the premium nature of the combined skills you offer. Remember, clients will pay more for professionals who can deliver not only technical solutions but also strategic insights that benefit their overall goals.

Taking Control of Your Career

It's vital to recognize that you have a choice in how you navigate your professional life. You can either be a commodity, producing standard work products, or seize control over your career by becoming a business development leader. This choice requires adopting the mindset and strategies of a seller-doer.

By actively engaging in all aspects of your work, fostering relationships, and emphasizing quality delivery, you will not only enhance your skill set but also significantly increase your value to both your current employer and future clients.

Your Path Forward

In conclusion, showcasing your value as a seller-doer is not merely about fulfilling your role; it requires a proactive approach to your career. Be involved, share ideas, and take ownership of your projects. By adopting these tactics, you can effectively control your workload, expand your influence, and elevate your professional standing. As you embrace these steps, remember that your potential to succeed lies in your hands—it's time to take the lead in your career!

Chapter Summary:

- Actively engage in team discussions to build deep professional relationships.

- Share your ideas and take the initiative to elevate project outcomes.

- Collaborate on proposals to build trust and credibility with clients.

- Deliver high-quality work consistently to enhance your professional reputation.

Chapter Twenty-Three

Top Three Actionable Takeaways for Immediate Impact

As an up-and-coming design professional, you might wonder how you can immediately impact your career. The road to becoming a successful seller-doer—someone who not only designs but also actively contributes to business development—might feel daunting at first, but don't worry! By focusing on just a few fundamental skills, you can take control of your workload and position yourself as an invaluable asset in your organization. Here are the top three actionable takeaways that you can implement right away to make a significant difference in your career.

1. Continue to Do Good Work

The foundation of any successful design career lies in the quality of your work. It's simple yet incredibly effective: when you produce exceptional designs and exceed expectations, you create a solid reputation for yourself. Your work becomes your calling card.

So, what does "good work" mean? It's more than just meeting deadlines or sticking to project specifications; it involves going above and beyond. Make sure your designs are not only visually appealing but also functional and client-focused. Always seek feedback and be open to constructive criticism. Remember, every project is an opportunity to learn and evolve your skills.

Building a portfolio filled with your best projects will serve as a testament to your abilities. This will not only provide you with a sense of accomplishment, but it will also attract potential clients and collaborators who value quality. Investing time in your craft will pay off in dividends as you establish yourself as a trusted professional.

2. Ask Real Questions and Practice Active Listening

One of the most powerful tools at your disposal is the ability to ask insightful questions. Throughout your journey in this book, we've discussed various questions you can pose to clients, colleagues, and stakeholders. These aren't just any questions; they are designed to dig deeper into their needs, challenges, and aspirations.

When you engage in conversations, practice active listening. This means truly focusing on what the other person is saying—without thinking about your response while they speak. Being present in the moment will equip you to better understand your client's wants and needs. This understanding will allow you to tailor your design solutions more effectively, distinguishing yourself from competitors who may not take the time to listen.

Let's illustrate this with a quick example. Imagine you're speaking with a potential client who has a vague idea of what they want. Instead of jumping straight to solutions, ask questions like, "What challenges are you facing with your current design?" or "How do you envision the end experience for your users?" These questions will open the door to deeper insights and position you as a thoughtful problem solver in their eyes.

3. Get Involved Beyond Your Daily Tasks

It's easy to fall into the routine of just showing up for work, completing your tasks, and going home. However, to truly thrive in the design industry, you need to step outside your daily responsibilities. Seeking opportunities to get involved in industry events, workshops, and networking sessions.

Building relationships is key. Connect not just with potential clients, but also with other professionals—sub-consultants, teaming partners, and even competitors. Engage with individuals who share your core values. Building a network of like-minded professionals can open doors to collaborations that will enhance your career and broaden your horizons.

Don't forget to consider the values that matter to you. Aligning yourself with partners who share your ethical and professional standards will create a more fulfilling work environment and lead to stronger, more effective collaborations. It's not just about who you know, but also about how closely your values align with your professional circle.

Focus on Communication Skills

While the three takeaways emphasized above are crucial, let's not forget about the power of effective communication. In your role, you will often need to articulate complex ideas in a clear, relatable manner. As you develop your projects and relationships, work on improving your communication skills—both written and verbal.

Avoid jargon and technical terms that might alienate clients or collaborators who are not as familiar with your field. Instead, focus on storytelling. Every project has a narrative; be that narrative's champion. Share not only what you did but why you did it, and how it benefits the client or user. This approach will better engage your audience and help you prove your claims.

Just a Few Key Skills Go a Long Way

As we wrap up, remember that thriving in the design industry doesn't require a laundry list of advanced skills. Instead, concentrate your energy on a few effective practices: doing quality work, posing the right questions, engaging with your industry, and communicating clearly.

Practice these skills relentlessly. Develop them incrementally, seeking small wins along the way. You'll discover that success in your career is not some unattainable goal, but a series of deliberate and focused efforts. By concentrating on these actionable takeaways, you will position yourself as a sought-after design professional who is not only competent in their craft but also valuable to the business world.

So, what's stopping you? Take control today, implement these strategies, and watch your impact grow!

Chapter Summary:

- Deliver high-quality designs consistently to build your professional reputation.

- Ask insightful questions and actively listen to understand client needs.

- Engage in industry events to expand your network and create valuable connections.

- Improve your communication skills to present ideas clearly and effectively.

Chapter Twenty-Four

The Future of Business Development in Engineering and Construction

As an up-and-coming design professional in the engineering and construction fields, you may be curious about what the future holds, especially regarding business development and sales. Understanding how the landscape is evolving now can empower you to take charge of your workload and position yourself as a valuable "seller-doer." In this chapter, we will explore the expected changes in business development, the enduring fundamentals that remain constant, and the practical steps you can take to ensure your success.

Understanding the Evolving Landscape

Imagine the engineering and construction industry as a vast, ever-changing landscape—much like a city skyline that continuously evolves with new buildings, technologies, and regulations. This evolution can seem daunting, but understanding the key trends will help you navigate this complexity. Projects are increasingly using technologies like artificial intelligence, drones, and advanced materials, and regulations are constantly shifting to address environmental and safety concerns.

For beginners, it's essential to grasp that although the tools and methods may change, the fundamentals of business development remain unaltered. This means that no matter how complicated new projects might become, the essence of successful business development is always about building relationships and understanding the needs of your clients.

Relationship Building: The Core of Business Development

In engineering and construction, business development depends heavily on relationships. Think of it like planting a garden. You must nourish the seeds (your relationships) through communication, trust, and empathy to watch them grow into fruitful partnerships. Here are some actionable steps you can take:

1. **Engage with Clients Regularly**: Make it a habit to check in with clients, even when you're not actively pursuing a project. Simple gestures like sending updates, sharing industry insights, or asking for feedback keep you top-of-mind and build camaraderie.

2. **Listen Actively**: Understand that your clients face various challenges—both technical and non-technical. Make it a priority to listen

to their needs. This practice will not only help you identify solutions, but also reinforce the trust they place in you.

3. **Network Strategically**: Attend industry events, seminars, or local meet-ups. Use these platforms to connect with other professionals. The more people you know, the more potential partnerships you create.

Identifying Challenges and Offering Solutions

New technologies and complex regulations will shape the challenges your clients face. Identifying these obstacles and addressing them will set you apart as an invaluable asset.

1. **Stay Informed**: Keep abreast of the latest industry news, trends, and emerging technologies. This vigilance will position you as a knowledgeable partner to your clients. You can subscribe to industry publications or join relevant online forums.

2. **Consultative Approach**: When discussing project challenges, adopt a consultative approach. Ask questions that help uncover deeper issues, demonstrating your dedication to solving their problems—not just your own.

3. **Positioning Your Team**: Build a team that is equipped to handle both technical and non-technical problems. By understanding diverse skill sets and how they contribute to a project, you can assemble a team that tackles your clients' challenges effectively.

Mastering Conflict Resolution

In a world where projects become increasingly complex, the potential for conflict also rises. Learning how to navigate these conflicts gracefully can strengthen your relationships and your reputation in the industry.

1. **Communicate Transparently**: Be open about any challenges faced during a project. Clients appreciate honesty and will proba-

bly feel more secure knowing there is transparency throughout the process.

2. **Seek Common Ground**: When conflicts arise, aim to understand all parties' perspectives. Find common ground and focus on solutions that address the bigger picture.

3. **Document Agreements**: Whenever you agree or resolution, document it. This record helps prevent misunderstandings and provides a reference for future interactions.

Tracking Success and Building a Reputation

In business development, demonstrating success is essential. Your reputation as a reliable seller depends on your ability to deliver consistently.

1. **Collect Testimonials**: After completing a project, ask for feedback or testimonials. Positive remarks from clients can be an influential marketing tool for your next project.

2. **Analyze Project Outcomes**: Review completed projects to identify successes and areas for improvement. Use these insights to enhance future projects and refine your approach to business development.

3. **Cultivate Long-Term Relationships**: Remember, business development is a marathon, not a sprint. Consistently take steps to nurture your relationships, and they will likely pay off in future projects.

The Importance of Team Loyalty

As you embark on your career, understand that effective business development is also about the people you work with. Building loyal teams can amplify your success.

1. **Foster a Collaborative Environment**: Encourage teamwork and open communication within your team. The more collaborative your team is, the stronger your projects will be.

2. **Value Contributions**: Show appreciation for your team's efforts. Recognizing individual contributions fosters loyalty and motivates your team to excel in their roles.

3. **Offer Development Opportunities**: Invest in your team's professional growth by providing training or mentorship opportunities. This not only enhances your team's capabilities but also reinforces their commitment to the organization's success.

Start Now to Prepare for the Future

Embracing the changes in business development isn't just about reacting to complexity—it's about proactively preparing for it. As we've discussed, the future landscape will continue to grow more complicated with new challenges.

By focusing on building strong relationships and mastering the art of problem-solving now, you'll equip yourself to navigate future complexities with ease. Starting this journey—whether through networking, learning, or practicing empathy—will make the challenges ahead seem less daunting.

Conclusion

In closing, the future of business development in engineering and construction is poised for transformation. For you, the aspiring seller-doer, this change offers an exciting opportunity to define your role and influence the success of your projects. The core values of relationship-building, understanding client challenges, and fostering loyalty will never go out of style.

As the complexities of your work increase, remember that starting now is more helpful than waiting. By investing in your skills and relationships today, you position yourself as an invaluable asset in an evolving industry. So take those steps—embrace the uncertainty, and prepare to thrive in the future of business development!

Chapter Summary:

- Engage regularly with clients to build trust and long-lasting relationships.

- Stay informed about industry trends to proactively address client challenges.

- Master conflict resolution through transparent communication and seeking common ground.

- Cultivate team loyalty by fostering collaboration and valuing contributions.

Chapter Twenty-Five

Thriving as a Seller-Doer

Where to Connect for Insights on Business Development

To excel as a design professional in the evolving engineering and construction industries, forming the right connections is crucial. Networking through organizations like the **American Public Works Association (APWA)** and the **American Society of Civil Engineers (ASCE)** is a great starting point. Attending their workshops, conferences, and seminars exposes you to industry leaders and like-minded professionals who share your ambition.

Beyond professional organizations, online platforms like LinkedIn are invaluable for expanding your network. By following industry leaders, joining discussion groups, and engaging with relevant content, you position yourself in the midst of critical conversations that shape your field.

Local chapters and meetups also provide opportunities to learn about regional challenges and trends, often leading to collaborations sparked during casual conversations. Additionally, engaging in webinars and online discussions hosted by these groups can deepen your expertise and create avenues for active learning.

For tailored guidance, turn to resources like **Waldrop Communications** and **BradleyWaldrop.com**. Waldrop Communications provides tools for marketing and mastering business development skills, while BradleyWaldrop.com offers personal insights and leadership strategies designed to bolster your professional acumen.

Key Takeaways:

- Join industry organizations like APWA and ASCE.
- Attend local and national networking events.
- Use platforms like LinkedIn to expand your reach.
- Leverage resources like Waldrop Communications for tailored business development strategies.

The Power of Building Genuine Relationships

At the heart of effective business development is relationship-building. Strong, genuine connections with clients and stakeholders form the foundation of long-term success. The cornerstone of this process is **active listening**—engaging fully with your client to uncover their true needs, preferences, and challenges.

Instead of focusing solely on selling your solutions, practice asking thoughtful, open-ended questions like, "What specific outcomes are you hoping to achieve with this project?" This approach not only builds trust but also demonstrates your commitment to tailoring your solutions to their needs.

Trust is the currency of relationships and is earned through consistent communication and reliability. Deliver on your commitments and address challenges transparently, proving that you are a dependable partner invested in the client's success.

Tailoring your approach to each client further strengthens relationships. Aligning your team's expertise with a client's specific goals—such as incorporating sustainability into designs—shows you're paying attention and creating bespoke solutions.

Key Takeaways:
- Build trust through active listening and thoughtful communication.
- Tailor your approach to individual client needs.
- Position yourself as a collaborator, not just a service provider.
- Strong relationships lead to repeat business, candid feedback, and career growth.

The Future of Business Development: Becoming a Seller-Doer

The modern engineering and construction industries demand professionals who can combine technical expertise with business acumen. This dual role, known as a **seller-doer**, positions you as both a designer and a driver of business growth. Embracing this role requires developing skills in proposal writing, negotiation, and relationship-building.

Start by exploring resources like **"The Lean Startup" by Eric Ries** and **"How to Win Friends and Influence People" by Dale Carnegie** to cultivate an entrepreneurial mindset. Online platforms such as Coursera and LinkedIn Learning also offer courses on critical skills like crafting compelling proposals.

Mentorship is another key to success. A mentor can provide personalized advice on navigating the nuances of business development and identifying the best opportunities within your field.

To influence hiring and project decisions within your organization, build strong relationships with operational teams. By understanding their priorities and aligning with them, you can position yourself as a key player in securing valuable projects.

Professional development activities like proposal-writing workshops, networking events, and coaching programs tailored for seller-doers provide practical tools to boost your confidence and effectiveness.

Key Takeaways:
- Equip yourself with business skills through books and courses.

- Seek mentorship to gain insider knowledge and guidance.

- Build relationships within your organization to influence critical decisions.

- Engage in coaching programs and professional workshops.

The Roadmap to Success

Combining these insights into a cohesive strategy can transform your career. By focusing on connecting with industry resources, building genuine relationships, and adopting the seller-doer mindset, you'll position yourself as an invaluable professional in your field.

Take proactive steps today:

1. Join relevant industry organizations.

2. Engage in online and in-person networking opportunities.

3. Sharpen your skills with targeted books and courses.

4. Seek mentorship and coaching tailored to your goals.

Success in business development is not just about technical capability—it's about your ability to connect, relate, and lead. Start building your future as a seller-doer today and watch your career soar.

Chapter Twenty-Six

Unlock Your Proposal Success with Our FREE Cheat Sheet!

Are you an up-and-coming design engineer struggling to craft cover letters that *capture* attention? Do you find yourself facing ***writer's block*** when it comes to communicating your unique value? You're not alone!

Introducing the Professional's Proposal Cover Letter Cheat Sheet!

This essential resource is here to catapult your proposals from *ordinary* to *extraordinary* in just minutes.

Here's What You'll Gain:

- **Instant Connection**: Learn the proven techniques to quickly establish rapport with your clients, even on the most politically charged projects. Your words will resonate, making your proposal stand out from the clutter.

- **Distinctive Differentiation**: Discover how to effectively showcase what sets your services apart from the competition. No more blending in—**your proposals will shine!**

- **Writer's Block No More**: Our cheat sheet guides you step-by-step, ensuring that you never hit a wall when writing. You'll have the confidence to deliver compelling cover letters every time.

Don't Let Your Competition Leave You in the Dust!

Whether you're looking to land that dream project or secure a lucrative contract, the Professional's Proposal Cover Letter Cheat Sheet is your **secret weapon** for success.

Ready to elevate your proposals? It's your moment to shine!

Act Now! Visit waldropcommunications.com/cover-letter-cheatsheet to download your FREE cheat sheet today and watch your professional relationships flourish!

Start crafting proposals that captivate and convert—**because your success deserves the best!**

www.ingramcontent.com/pod-product-compliance
Lightning Source LLC
Chambersburg PA
CBHW071604220526
45469CB00003B/1115